hooked on CROCHET

20 Sassy Projects

Candi Jensen

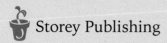
Storey Publishing

The mission of Storey Publishing is to serve our customers by publishing practical
information that encourages personal independence in harmony with the environment.

Edited by Gwen Steege, Siobhan Dunn, Sarah Guare
Art direction by Lisa Clark
Cover and text design by Susi Oberhelman
Text production by Cindy McFarland
Cover photographs by © John Dolan: back left and back right;
© Kevin Kennefick: spine, © Ross Whitaker: front, back center
Interior photographs by © John Dolan: 2, 4, 5 left and right, 6 center and right,
43, 44, 47, 48, 55, 56, 59, 60, 62, 64, 72, 81, 83, 84, 93, 94, 102, 107, 108,
111, 112, 115, 116, 125, 126, 129, 133, 134, 137, 138; © Kevin Kennefick:
1, 3, 11, 12–13, 15-17, 36, 39–40, 50, 61, 66, 68–69, 73, 76, 80, 86, 91, 94,
95, 98, 103, 104–105, 119, 121, 122, 130, 135; © Ross Whitaker: 5 center,
6 left, 8, 63, 71, 75, 97, 101
How-to illustrations by Brigita Fuhrmann
Project schematics by Ilona Sherratt
Indexed by Susan Olason, Indexes & Knowledge Maps

Text copyright © 2004 by Candi Jensen

The information in this book is true and complete to the best of our knowledge.
All recommendations are made without guarantee on the part of the author
or Storey Publishing. The author and publisher disclaim any liability in
connection with the use of this information. For additional information, please contact
Storey Publishing, 210 MASS MoCA Way, North Adams, MA 01247.

Storey books are available for special premium and promotional uses and for
customized editions. For further information, please call 1-800-793-9396.

Printed in China by Regent Publishing Services
10 9 8 7 6 5 4 3

Library of Congress Cataloging-in-Publication Data
Jensen, Candi.
Hooked on crochet : 20 sassy projects / Candi Jensen.
p. cm.
Includes index.
ISBN-13: 978-1-58017-547-0 (alk. paper)
ISBN-10: 1-58017-547-3 (alk. paper)
1. Crocheting–Patterns. I. Title.
TT825.J48 2004
746.43'4041–dc22

2004001517

Dedication

To my husband, Tom, who makes me laugh.

Acknowledgments

When an idea goes from conception to finished project,
there are many people to help guide it along. Without my support network,
this book would not have been possible.

First I want to thank my extra set of hands and brains, Joyce Nordstrom.
She always knows how to take any design I might come up with and make it work. Joyce has
become much more than just a helping hand — she is a trusted friend. I also want to thank
Judy Timmer and Jane Lind for their expert crocheting and the long hours
they put into finishing many of the projects in this book.

Thanks to my supportive family for helping me make it through the long hours
and giving me encouragement. Hugs to my son, Jonathan, for hanging in there;
my daughter, Heather, who is creative and beautiful; my son-in-law, John, who is sweet
and kind and without whom I wouldn't have one of the best gifts there is, my grandson,
Johnny. Kisses to my mom, Jean, for passing on her creativity
and to my sister, Rajeana, for her unyielding support.

Many thanks to the creative staff at Storey Publishing who have made my work
look beautiful, especially Lisa Clark for her outstanding art direction; Brigita Fuhrmann
for clear and precise drawings; Susi Oberhelman for book design; Cindy McFarland for
page layout; John Dolan, Ross Whitaker, and Kevin Kennefick for their photography; and
Wendy Scofield for photo styling. A special thank you to Siobhan Dunn for always being
cheerful and positive and making me sound good. And last but not least, I want to thank
Gwen Steege, who has not only become a friend but has also taught me so much about
myself and about the art of writing a book.

CONTENTS

Get Hooked   9

Pick Up Your Hook   36

Cell Phone and Eyeglass Cases • 38
Basic Scarf • 42
Swinging Ribbon Bag • 46

Now Add Color   50

Bamboo Handle Purse • 54
Striped Skinny Scarf • 58
Striped Throw Pillow • 62

Shaping Up   66

Little Black Wrap • 70
Lacy Sleeveless Shell • 74
Candy Stripe Baby Sweater • 78
The Swimsuit Issue Bikini • 82

Not Your Granny's Square   86

Posies for Tanks • 92
Red-Hot Granny Square Scarf • 96
Mohair Flapper Hat • 100

Completely Hooked   104

Posh Frock • 106
Designer Jacket • 110
Chic Hippie Skirt • 114
Be Jeweled • 118

Hooking Your Nest   122

Vintage Embellishments • 124
Diamond Square Pillow • 128
Antique Lampshade Fringe • 132
Lazy-Afternoon Hammock • 136

CROCHET BASICS FOR LEFTIES   140

RESOURCES   142

INDEX   143

Get Hooked

Crochet is easy. Really. You may look at the patterns and projects in this book and think to yourself that you won't be able to pull them off, but you know what? You can. Crochet's just a hook, some yarn, and a series of loops and knots that, worked in the right sequence, turn into something quite beautiful.

You might also have a misconception about what crochet looks like. Most people think of crochet as dowdy old doilies (although even those can be cool if done in the right colors) and ill-fitting sweaters that Grandma forced you to wear as a child. One look at the projects in this book and that paradigm will shift about 180 degrees. Crochet is in all the fashion magazines as well as on the runways in New York and Paris, although you may not have noticed that what the models were wearing was indeed crocheted. Crochet is fun, it's easy and it's fashionable, and I know you'll enjoy doing it!

As you work your way through this book, take your time, don't feel pressured to be perfect the first time you crochet, and, above all else, enjoy yourself. My goal isn't to get all tedious about it and preach to you about the right way to crochet. It shouldn't be a dreaded chore. I hope that instead you'll find it's a creative way to spend your time.

Crochet is very forgiving, and so am I. I don't care how you hold the yarn — just find a way that's comfortable for you. The same goes for the hook; whatever works best for you will probably get the job done. Remember, there are no "crochet police" standing over your shoulder. If you already crochet, then the patterns in this book will delight you; if you learned to crochet once upon a time and never kept up with it because all the projects you found were for toilet paper cozies, then this book will be a revelation. I firmly believe you'll be inspired and excited by how far crochet has come and the many wonderful things you can do with it.

FIRST THINGS FIRST

The few things you need to begin crocheting are basically a hook and some yarn. You also need to know standard terms and abbreviations in order to follow a pattern. I call this the "Language of Crochet," but don't worry, you won't have to learn to conjugate verbs! I'll walk you through the basic equipment and lingo, and go through a pattern so it doesn't look so complicated and foreign. Then I'll teach you to crochet step-by-step. Let's get started because the best way to learn crochet is to do it.

The Hook

Although there are several different types of crochet hooks, they all have one thing in common, a hook at the end. Most hooks are made of either aluminum, plastic, or wood. Very small steel hooks are usually used with thread to make lace and for fine detail work, and although we don't cover them in this book, it's a good idea to familiarize yourself with all the hooks and their uses.

You catch and manipulate the yarn with the *head*, which is located at the end of your crochet hook. Behind the head is the *shank*, followed by a flat portion that is called the *grip*, and finally the *handle*. The flat portion is where you place your fingers to control the hook (hence the "grip"). Steel hooks sometimes have a thicker plastic handle that makes them easier to grip.

Diagram of a Hook

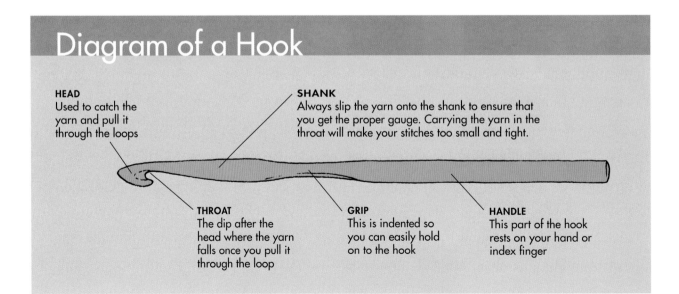

HEAD
Used to catch the yarn and pull it through the loops

SHANK
Always slip the yarn onto the shank to ensure that you get the proper gauge. Carrying the yarn in the throat will make your stitches too small and tight.

THROAT
The dip after the head where the yarn falls once you pull it through the loop

GRIP
This is indented so you can easily hold on to the hook

HANDLE
This part of the hook rests on your hand or index finger

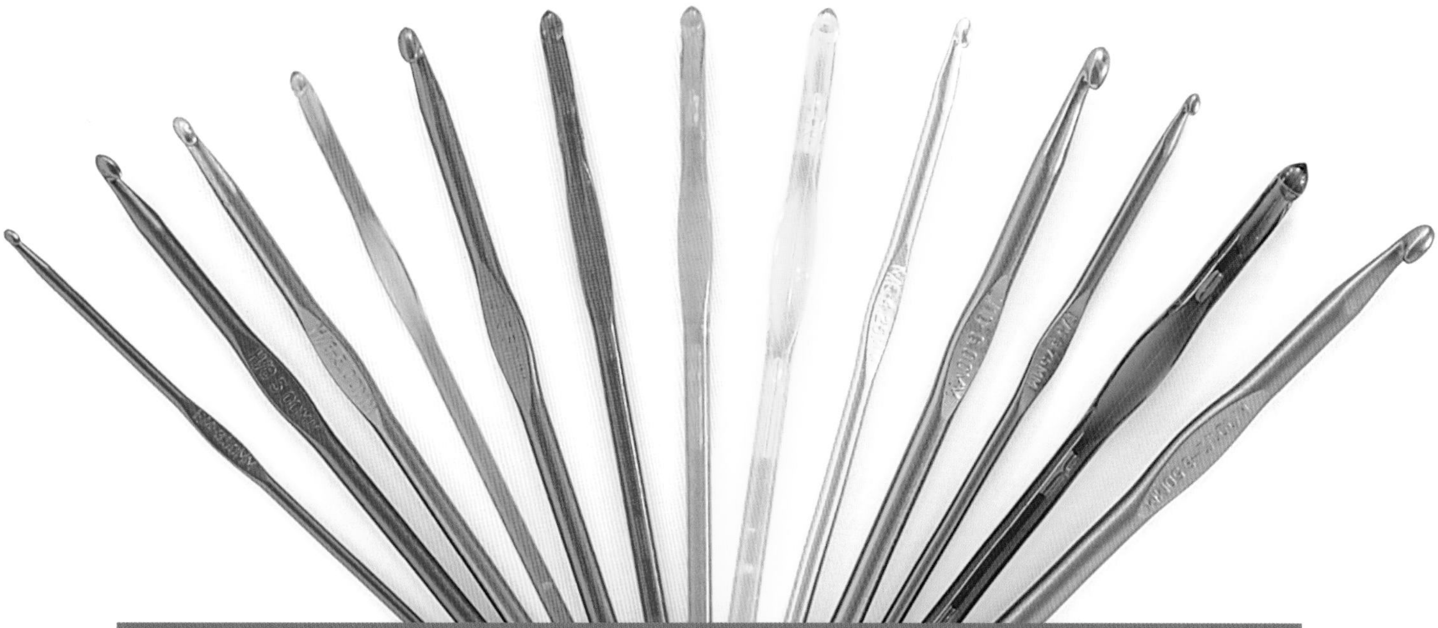

Hook Conversion

There is little standardization to crochet hooks, so you might find that they differ from manufacturer to manufacturer. It is always best to experiment with your yarn and whatever hook is called for to see if you can get the proper gauge* for the pattern.

- In the U.S., hooks are sized in either letters, B through S, or numbers, 1 through 16.
- In the metric and English equivalents (see conversion chart at the right), only numbers are used. In the patterns in this book we give both the U.S. sizes and the metric equivilent.
- When you start a project, you'll see that the pattern always calls for a certain-size hook. This is really only a starting point, but more about that when we talk about gauge.
- Standard hook size refers to aluminum and plastic hooks, but crochet hooks can be wood or bone, and they usually follow the same sizing standards.

*To learn what gauge is, turn to page 23.

Approximate Hook Sizes

U.S. (American)	CONTINENTAL (metric)	U.K. (English)
B/1	2.5 mm	12
C/2	3 mm	11
D/3	3.25 mm	10
E/4	3.5 mm	9
F/5	4 mm	8
G/6	4.25 mm	7
7	4.5 mm	7
H/8	5 mm	6
I/9	5.5 mm	5
J/10	6 mm	4
K/10.5	7 mm	3
L/11	8 mm	-
M/13	9 mm	-
N/15	10 mm	-
P/16	15 mm	-
Q	16 mm	-
S	19 mm	-

Yarn

What can I say — I love yarn! It's my prime motivation for becoming a knitwear designer. I love the colors and textures as well as just running it through my fingers when I crochet. Nothing is better than walking into a yarn store and seeing rows and rows of fabulous yarn. As you get more into crochet, you too could become a yarnophile. But enough about me and my addiction. The important thing for you to know is that certain types of yarn work better for certain projects. As you learn how yarn works, this will seem more relevant. For now, you'll have to trust me that the main reason to use the yarn suggested by the pattern is that it will give the result closest to the one in the photo. This might seem obvious, but it's tempting to make projects in other colors and fibers, so it helps if you know something about the characteristics of the many available yarns.

PLANT FIBERS

The two basic types of yarn are natural fibers and synthetics. Natural fibers comprise both animal fibers and vegetable fibers. Rayon, which is a by-product of wood and cotton, is in essence a natural fiber but because it is man-made, it's considered a synthetic. Yarns made from plant fibers share many qualities — primarily strength and durability.

COTTON

I love cotton and use it a lot in my designs, and not just because I live in California. It's really well suited to crochet. There are many different types of cotton plants and each one gives us a different

yarn. The softest and most sought after are Egyptian and Sea Island cottons. They both produce a fine, luxurious, long-staple fiber. A cross between these two fibers gives us Pima cotton. The longer the staple on the cotton fiber, the stronger the yarn made out of it will be. Cotton is not as elastic as wool and it tends to stretch, so it's often mixed with wool or acrylic to give it more elasticity. Mercerized cotton is produced by treating cotton in a bath of caustic soda, which makes the fibers stronger and gives them a sheen. Cotton is extremely durable and readily absorbs dye, allowing for great color intensity and variety.

SILK

Silk is spun on an itsy-bitsy filament that extrudes from silkworms. Round and round they spin their cocoons, producing a continuous filament that can be 1,600 yards long. To get the silk, you actually unravel that filament. It's no wonder silk is so coveted. Silk can be found in the wild by picking cocoons from mulberry trees, but it's more likely to be cultivated. The long continuous filaments are used in finer, lustrous silks, while the cocoons with holes in them are chopped up and made into what we refer to as "raw silk." Silk is strong and, contrary to what most of us think, very washable.

LINEN

Linen also comes from a plant, and there is evidence that it has been around since cavemen. It is made from the flax plant, which may seem harsh, but you know, necessity is the mother of invention and all! To prepare it for spinning, you have to soak flax and then beat the living daylights out of it, but once spun, it is a strong, silky yarn. It's not very resilient, and is usually blended with other yarns to make it softer and easier to work with. It also wrinkles easily (can't you just imagine the cavewomen trying to iron out their wrinkles) but this is not so much of an issue in crocheted fabrics.

ANIMAL FIBERS

Any yarn that is spun from animal fur, hair, or fleece falls into this category.

WOOL

Of all the natural fibers, wool is the most common. Spun from the fleece of sheep, it's warm and resilient, and it easily absorbs water. Its fiber makes it easy to work with and very durable. Different types of wool depend on the type and age of the sheep it comes from. Lamb's wool comes from the first shearing of the sheep (you guessed it) and is very soft. Merino sheep have long, soft coats, which makes merino wool expensive and coveted. Shetland wool, which originally came from the sheep of the Shetland Islands, has become a generic term for any fine soft wool.

Wool fiber has tiny scales on it that cause it to bind together when put into hot water and agitated. In some instances, this can be a good thing, like when making a felted project. So how can we have "machine-washable" wool? Well, the fiber is coated with acrylic so the wool scales don't bond together when subjected to a hot tub. So, is it still a natural fiber? We probably don't want to open up that hornet's nest! For our purposes, you just need to know how to wash the yarn you are using and what it feels like against your skin.

Wool is also used extensively in blends with other fibers, such as cotton, acrylic, and silk. It is easily dyed and comes in many, many colors.

MOHAIR

Mohair comes from angora goats (which, by the way, have nothing to do with angora fiber). Mohair has a "hairy" look and is usually blended with wool or nylon to give it stability. Although mohair yarn looks incredibly fine, because of its hairiness you usually crochet with it fairly loosely, using a large hook. Otherwise you end up with a dense, matted fabric — probably a little like the goat. Mohair takes dye well and is available in beautiful colors.

CASHMERE

While we're on the subject of goats, let's talk about cashmere, which comes from cashmere goats. Who would have guessed that goats could be such luxury objects? You'll never again look at them the same way! The goat's belly is combed once a year to get the soft, downlike fiber. Oh, and the goat lives only in the mountains of China and Tibet — now you know why it's so expensive. Because cashmere is just the fine down of the goat, the fibers aren't very long. It is generally spun with other fibers — most commonly wool.

ANGORA

Remember that angora goat? Well, angora yarn comes not from the goat but from the angora rabbit. The softest fibers are combed from the rabbit, not shorn. Because the fiber is fairly short and hard to spin on its own, it is usually blended with wool or other fibers.

ALPACA AND CAMEL

These two are grouped together because they're close relatives. The alpaca is actually a member of the camel family (although I don't think they keep in touch). Both camel and alpaca have long lustrous fibers that make soft yarns. They are difficult to dye, so most alpaca is bleached before dyeing, and camel is usually found only in its natural color.

SYNTHETICS

Don't let synthetics scare you. Possibly you associate them with polyester leisure suits or strangely colored afghans, but they really do have a place in the yarn hierarchy. For one thing, they're usually easy to care for and can be thrown in the washer and dryer. They are also great when blended with natural fibers. Besides, synthetics have come a

long way since the leisure suit era. Developed after WWII, synthetic fibers are made from by-products of coal and petroleum (I know that sounds weird). When blended with other fibers, they pass on their best attributes — making cotton and silk more elastic and wool washable.

Another term you may encounter on a yarn label is *microfiber*, which can encompass anything from branded names like Tencel and Lycra to plain old elastic. These fibers are appearing in more yarn blends for added strength, warmth, and elasticity.

ACRYLIC

Acrylic is supposed to imitate the properties of wool. It has the same resilience and can have a similar look, but it lacks the warmth of wool. It dyes well and comes in a wide range of colors. It is less expensive to produce than natural fiber yarn, and therefore tends to cost less. It is used widely in blends.

NYLON

Nylon is actually the manufacturer's name for polyamide, but it is now used to describe any polyamide fiber. It's the strongest of the manmade fibers, which is why it's used in carpeting. You won't find unadulterated nylon fiber on the market, but it's added to other yarns all the time, especially novelty yarns, to give them extra strength and to hold the fibers together.

NOVELTY YARNS

This is a generic term used to refer to all those yarns that have bumps, slumps, metallic threads, or other mixed media woven in. Because it covers a lot of different yarns, I've bunched them together to help define them. Novelty yarns have recently become very popular, though they've been on the market for at least 20 years. They're usually either a heavier-weight or a thin, almost threadlike yarn. Most shouldn't be used when you want a pattern to be visible. Novelty blends with mohair or "fur" (sometimes referred to as "eyelash" yarns) are great for quick, simple projects, such as scarves. They tend to be a little harder to work with because of the different textures and added elements, but the end results can be really fun and unique.

Weight and Ply

Once you start learning about yarns, you'll want to know about their weight and thickness. Then there is ply, which has to do with the way the strands of yarn are twisted together as well as how many strands have been used. Unravel a bit of yarn and look closely to examine its makeup and twist.

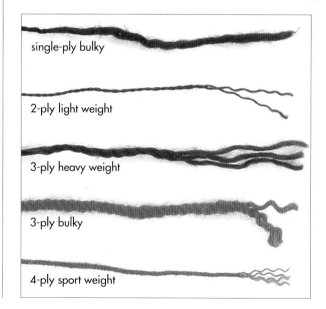

single-ply bulky

2-ply light weight

3-ply heavy weight

3-ply bulky

4-ply sport weight

Language of Crochet

Probably the most difficult thing about learning to crochet isn't the technique but the shorthand that is used in most patterns. At first glance, it looks as if the designer has an aversion to vowels, but, in fact, directions are filled with abbreviations that are used to make a pattern seem shorter. Don't let this intimidate you. It's really worthwhile knowing how to use the abbreviations right from the beginning, since you'll find them in most patterns and part of learning to crochet is learning to follow a pattern so that you can actually make stuff. Refer to the list on the facing page whenever you feel brain fatigue and can't remember what "sc" means. One of the most helpful pieces of advice I can think of is to make a copy of this list and keep it with whatever pattern you are working on.

In Your Bag

I'm assuming you're quickly going to learn to crochet and just love it so much you'll start doing it everywhere, in which case you'll need what we experts refer to as a crochet bag. Here are some things you'll want to stash there:

- Crochet hooks, sizes F through I (it's sometimes helpful to have a smaller hook for weaving in ends).
- Yarn
- Safety pins
- Large-eye yarn needle
- Sharp sewing scissors
- Tape measure and ruler
- List of abbreviations and a photocopy of the pattern you are working on

TERMS

Some of the crochet terms that you will run into are not abbreviated, but they still are a kind of shorthand that means something very specific.

Front loop. The loop closest to you at the top of the stitch

Back loop. The loop on the other side of the stitch

Post. The vertical area of the stitch

Right side. The side of your piece that will show

Wrong side. The back side of the piece

Right-hand side. The side on the right as you are looking at it while crocheting

Left-hand side. The side on the left as you are looking at it while crocheting

Work even. Follow the pattern as it has been established

Yarn over. Wrap the yarn around the hook from back to front

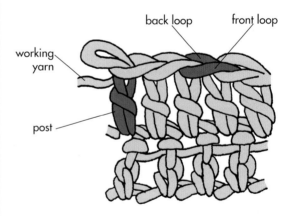

Two rows of double crochet

SYMBOLS

, ✷, † Asterisks, stars, and daggers are used to mark the beginning of a set of steps that you will need to repeat or work more than once. In the following example, you would follow the steps between the "" and the ";" twice.

Example

*Single crochet in the next 2 stitches, skip 1 stitch, single crochet in the next 2 stitches; repeat from * one more time.

( ), [ ] Parentheses or brackets are often used to enclose a set of steps within another set of steps. In the next example, the steps within parentheses are all worked in one of the chain stitches. The entire sequence is worked three times.

Example

* Work 3 double crochet in the next chain 1 space, chain 1, work (3 double crochet, chain 2, 3 double crochet) in next chain 2 space, chain 1; repeat from * 2 more times.

GAUGE

I'm going to tell you a little about gauge here, even though you don't actually know how to crochet yet. For more about gauge, see page 23.

Before you start any project, you have to check your gauge. I can't stress this enough and it should become your mantra when you learn to crochet. Gauge is the number of stitches and rows per inch, and it determines the finished measurement of your work. Since most patterns tell you what size hook and yarn to use, it's easy to skip over the gauge and just go for what they call for. But I can tell you from experience that you may have a slightly different way of holding the hook or yarn from how the designer does and that can affect your size dramatically. Checking gauge takes only a few minutes and is well worth the time and effort. Remember, before you start any project, check your gauge!

Abbreviations

alt	alternate	
beg	begin, beginning	
bl(s)	back loop, back loops	(see facing page)
cc	contrasting color	
ch(s)	chain, chains	(p. 22)
dc(s)	double crochet, double crochets	(p. 26)
dc 2 tog	double crochet two together	
dec	decrease, decreasing	(p. 68)
fig	figure	
fl(s)	front loop, front loops	(see facing page)
hdc	half double crochet(s)	(p. 28)
hdc 2 tog	half double crochet two together	
inc	increase	(p. 69)
lp(s)	loop, loops	
patt	pattern	
prev	previous	
rem	remain, remaining	
rep	repeat, repeating	
rnd(s)	round, rounds	
sc(s)	single crochet, single crochets	(p. 24)
sc 2 tog	single crochet two together	
sk	skip	
sl	slip	
sl st(s)	slip stitch, slip stitches	(p. 69)
sp	space, spaces	
st(s)	stitch, stitches	
tch	turning chain	(p. 25)
tog	together	
tr(s)	triple crochet, triple crochets	(p. 30)
yo	yarn over	(see facing page)
	Crochet basics for lefties	(p. 140)

HOOKING UP

Finally, we get to the fun part — taking up that hook and yarn and actually beginning to crochet. My babysitter taught me to crochet when I was 7 years old because she thought it would keep me quiet. Little did she know what she was unleashing! I never felt comfortable with the way she held her yarn, so I sort of developed my own way. Feel free to experiment and find one that feels right to you. Once you've learned how to do a single crochet (sc), double crochet (dc), half double crochet (hdc), and triple crochet (tr), you will be able to do almost any crochet project. Of course, there are other little tidbits you still need to learn, such as how to make color changes and how to shape a garment. Still, you'll be pleasantly surprised at how much you can accomplish with just these four techniques.

Getting Started

For practice, use a medium hook, like a "G" or "H", which is easy to maneuver, and a smooth, worsted-weight yarn, like a 100% wool, so the hook will slide in and out of the loops easily and you can see the structure of the stitches. It's easier to see your stitches if you work with light-colored yarn. After just a little practice, you'll soon be able to crochet an actual project, so don't get frustrated; just try it a couple of times. You'll be amazed at how quickly you know what you're doing.

HOLDING THE HOOK

It's important to try not to hold the hook too tightly in your fingers — it won't run away. But you do need to hold on to it tightly enough to control it easily. The way you hold it is not unlike the way you hold your pen or a fork. You don't need to choke the life out of these tools, but you want them to work for you.

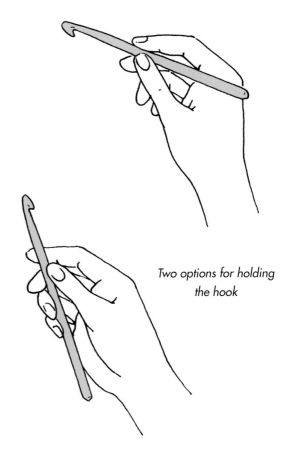

Two options for holding the hook

HOLDING THE YARN

There are many ways to hold the yarn, and once again it comes down to what feels right to you. I've given the two most common versions below.

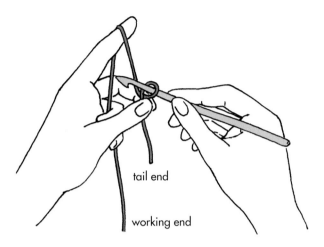

tail end

working end

Option 1: Loop the yarn over the index finger of your left hand. Hold the working end (the end coming from the skein or ball) loosely with the last two fingers of that hand. You can use these fingers to adjust the tension on the yarn as you draw the yarn along. Use your thumb and middle finger to hold the loop and tail of the yarn.

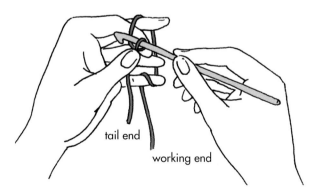

tail end

working end

Option 2: Wrap the yarn around the little finger of your left hand, then drape it over your middle finger. Use your thumb and index finger to hold the loop and tail of the yarn.

Slip Knot

Crochet begins with a single loop and then builds from there. Now that you have the hook and the yarn worked out, it's time to make that first loop.

1. Leaving a tail of about 6 inches, make a loop.

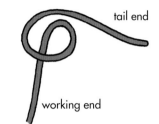

tail end

working end

2. With your crochet hook, reach through the loop and catch the tail end with the hook.

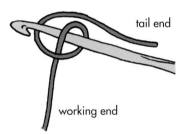

tail end

working end

3. Pull the yarn toward you through the loop.

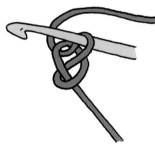

4. Tighten the knot on the hook.

Chain (ch)

Once you have a slip knot on your hook, you can start to build your structure. The building block for crochet is the beginning chain. Here's how it's done:

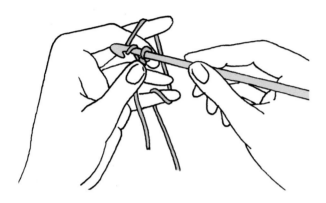

1. Bring the yarn over the hook from back to front, catch it with the hook, then pull it through the slip knot. It's important to slip the loop you've just made to the shank of the hook. If you leave it near the throat, the stitch will be too small.

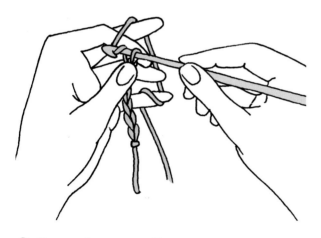

2. Repeat the process. Try to get a nice even tension. If you pull too hard, the chain will be too tight. If you don't give it enough tension, however, it will be too loose.

WORKING WITH THE CHAIN

Once you have the starting chain (ch), you can begin any of the basic stitches.

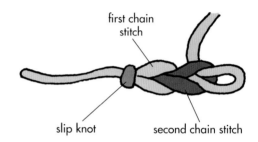

first chain stitch

slip knot

second chain stitch

Counting chains. When counting chains (chs), never count either the slip knot or the loop on the hook. To get the correct count, it helps to count the chains as you pull the loops through each time.

Front of a chain. Looks like a group of interlocking V's

Back of a chain. Looks like a series of bumps

All About Gauge

Making a gauge swatch is a good way to practice the stitches you're learning. Pattern directions always tell you to check your gauge. To do this, you simply crochet a swatch on which you can measure the number of stitches and rows you get within a certain width and length. You use the hook size and yarn indicated for the project, as well as the pattern stitch the project calls for. Complicated projects may have multiple pattern stitches, each one of which requires a gauge swatch, but you don't have to worry about multiple swatches in this book, as we're keeping things simple here.

For your sample swatch, use the yarn and hook you're practicing with. You're going to be working single crochet for this swatch, so you'll need to look ahead to the next page for single crochet directions. We're going to imagine that our pattern indicates a gauge of 20 stitches and 24 rows to a 4-inch square. To get the most accurate measurement, we'll crochet a swatch 6" by 6". This way, we can take the measurement an inch in from each side, because sometimes stitches near the edge aren't as even as stitches in the heart of the piece and thus distort the result.

Crocheting the Swatch

To begin, chain 31, then single crochet in the second loop from the hook and in each loop across the chain. (It's a good idea to count as you do this.) You should end up with 30 single crochets. Chain 1, turn your work, and single crochet in each stitch across. Go ahead and repeat these steps until your piece is about 6 inches long. End

by cutting the yarn and pulling it through the last loop.

Now, lay down the swatch, taking care not to stretch or pull it — you can't yank your gauge into submission! Lay a flat ruler over the swatch, with the end about an inch from the edge. Count the stitches within 4". If you got more than the 20 required stitches, try again with a larger hook size. If you got fewer stitches, try a smaller hook size. Don't forget to measure the rows per 4" as well; your goal is to get 24 rows. It's more important to get the exact same number of stitches and rows per 4 inches as the directions indicate than it is to use the hook size called for. This is why the hook requirements in pattern directions are usually followed by the note "or size needed to obtain gauge."

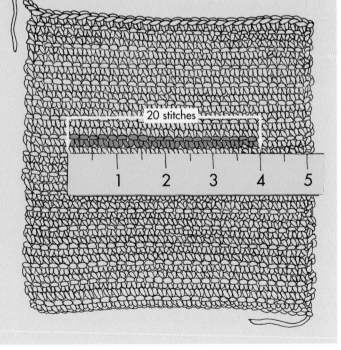

Single Crochet (sc)

Now that you're comfortable with the whole chain concept, let's start to learn some stitches. All crochet projects begin with a chain (ch), so you'll need to first chain (ch) 6 to practice the single crochet (sc). If you make a mistake, just pull out the stitches and start over. You aren't making anything yet — this is practice, and as I said, there are no crochet police watching you.

ROW 1

1. After making 6 chain stitches, begin the first row of single crochet by inserting the hook through the second chain from the hook.

2. Bring the yarn over the hook from the back to the front.

3. Pull the yarn to the front and move it to the shank of the hook. There are now two loops on the hook.

4. Bring the yarn over the hook again from back to front and pull it through both loops on the hook.

5. Now you have one loop on the hook, and you have completed 1 single crochet (sc).

6. Insert the hook into the next chain and repeat the process until you have reached the end of the chain. Do not crochet into the slip knot itself. You should see five stitches in the completed row. Don't forget to count as you work.

ROW 2

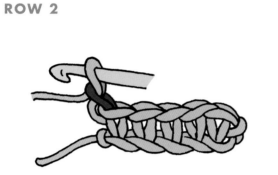

7. Before you turn to work a second row of single crochet, chain 1. This is called the *turning chain*. Now turn the piece counterclockwise so the back is facing you.

9. Continue in this way across the row and in subsequent rows until the piece is the desired length. You'll find it helps to count stitches as you work, so that you don't gain or lose any.

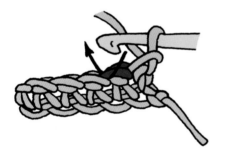

8. Work the first single crochet into the last single crochet of the previous row. This time, insert the hook under *both* top loops of the first single crochet and repeat steps 2–5.

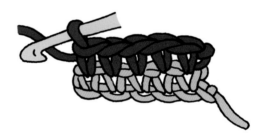

10. To end the piece, cut the yarn, leaving about a 6-inch tail, and then pull the yarn completely through the last loop.

Remember, as you work your first row of single crochet, it's important not to twist the chain, and always keep the front facing you.

Double Crochet (dc)

Double crochet (dc) is similar to single crochet (sc), only with a few more steps. Double crochet (dc) is a taller stitch, so you need to start with a chain that is a little longer. To practice, start with a chain of 12 stitches.

ROW 1

1. Bring the yarn over the hook from the back to the front. Insert the hook into the fourth chain from the hook.

2. Bring the yarn over the hook again, pull it through to the front, and move it to the shank of the hook. You now have three loops on the hook.

3. Bring the yarn over the hook again and draw it through the first two loops on the hook.

4. You now have two loops on the hook.

5. Bring the yarn over again from back to front and pull it through the two remaining loops on the hook.

6. You have now completed a double crochet.

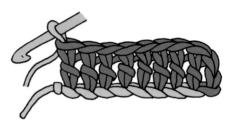

7. Repeat these steps 1–6 across the row, working in the next chain for each stitch.

ROW 2

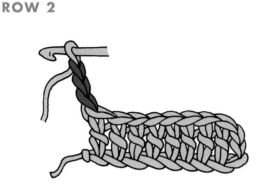

8. To work a second row, you need to turn your work and work back across the stitches as you did in the single crochet. But before you turn to work the second row, chain 3. This is the *turning chain* and it becomes the first stitch of the second row. You will need a turning chain at the end of each row.

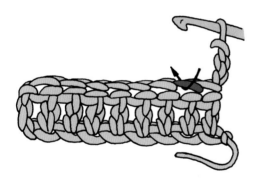

9. Turn the work counterclockwise. You will be inserting the hook into the top two loops of the stitches in this row. Yarn over from back to front, insert the hook into the second chain from hook, then repeat steps 2–6. Continue in this way, inserting the hook into each stitch to the end of the row.

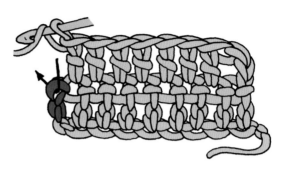

10. Insert the hook into the top of the last chain and complete your last double crochet.

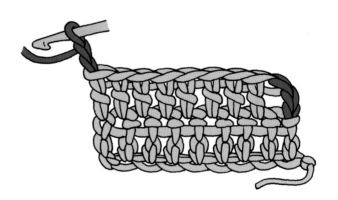

11. Chain 3 and turn as before. The last stitch in this and subsequent rows will be the turning chain. Always make your last double crochet in the top chain of the turning chain.

Half Double Crochet (hdc)

As the name implies, the half double crochet (hdc) takes one step out of the double crochet (dc), thereby making it a shorter stitch. It is also a little thicker because you are going through three loops at the same time. Once again, start with a chain of 12.

ROW 1

1. Bring the yarn over the hook from the back to the front. Insert the hook into the third chain from the hook.

2. Yarn over and draw the yarn through the chain to the front, then move it to the shank of the hook. You now have three loops on the hook.

3. Yarn over again from back to front and pull it through all three loops on the hook.

4. You have now completed a half double crochet.

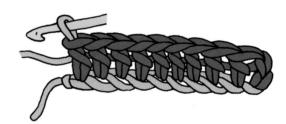

5. Repeat these steps in each chain across the row.

ROW 2

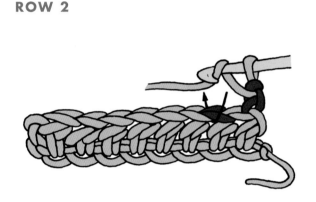

6. To work a second row of half double crochet, you need to turn your work and work back across the stitches as you did for double crochet. Before you turn your work, chain 2 (the turning chain). This becomes the first stitch of the second row and each row thereafter. Yarn over and insert the hook into the second stitch in the row.

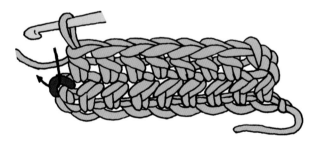

7. Repeat the steps for half double crochet across the row, working into both top loops of each stitch until you get to the chain 2 (turning chain) of the previous row.

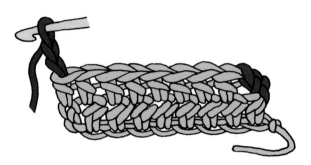

8. Insert the hook into the top chain of the turning chain and complete your last half double crochet. When you have completed the row, chain 2 and turn as before.

British Terms

The English have completely different terms for many crochet techniques, including stitches. If you are using a British pattern, these are some of the terms to watch out for.

U.S. TERM	U.K. TERM
single crochet (sc)	double crochet (dc)
half double crochet (hdc)	half treble (htr)
double crochet (dc)	treble (tr)
triple crochet (tr)	double treble (dtr)

Triple Crochet (tr)

The triple crochet (tr) is taller and has one step more than the double crochet (dc). Begin by chaining 11.

ROW 1

1. Bring the yarn over the hook twice from the back to the front.

2. Insert the hook into the fifth chain from the hook and yarn over.

3. Pull the yarn through the chain to the front and move it to the shank of the hook. You now have four loops on the hook.

4. Bring the yarn over again from back to front and pull it through the first two loops on the hook. You now have three loops on the hook.

5. Yarn over again. Pull the yarn through the next two loops on the hook.

6. You now have two loops on the hook.

7. Yarn over one more time and pull the yarn through the last two loops on the hook.

8. Repeat these steps across the row.

ROW 2

9. Before you turn your work, chain 4 (the turning chain). This will become the first stitch of the second row and each row hereafter.

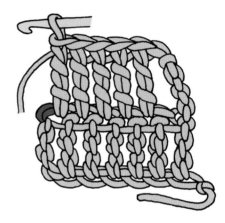

11. Insert the hook into the top chain of the turning chain and complete your last triple crochet.

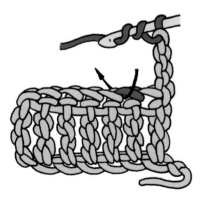

10. Yarn over twice and insert the hook under both loops of the second stitch from the hook. Repeat steps 3–7. Continue in this way, working into both top loops of each stitch across the row, until you get to the chain 4 (turning chain) of the previous row.

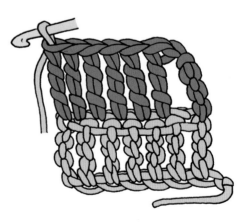

12. When you have completed the row, chain 4 and turn as before.

Joining a New Ball of Yarn

At some point you will finish a ball of yarn before you finish your project, and you'll need to add more yarn. Not to worry; joining yarn is easy. Whenever possible, do this at the beginning or end of a row, so you don't have stray strands in the middle of your work. If you notice that you are nearing the end of your yarn when you complete a row, make the join at the beginning of the next row rather than run out in the middle of the row. Here's how it's done:

Work until you have two loops left on the hook. Draw the new yarn through the two loops to finish the stitch using the new yarn. Leave 6-inch tails on both old and new yarns so that you can weave them into the wrong side later.

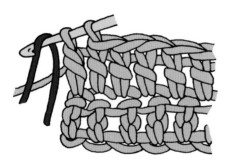

Joining new yarn

No Knots

You should never knot two ends of yarn together when crocheting. Not only does this create an unsightly bump or hole in the finished piece, but it almost always eventually pops through to the right side of the fabric — to reveal your shortcut!

Finishing

Once you complete a project, you need to know how to finish it properly. This entails not only sewing the pieces together and weaving in the loose ends of yarn, but also adding fringe or putting in a lining. It's tempting to put down your project, thinking you'll come back to it later, because this is a less glamorous part of the job. It can be tedious to weave in all the ends and intimidating to sew something together, but have heart: Neither procedure is really that bad. Plus, once you get the finishing touches over with, you'll be able to *use* your new hat or scarf or bikini or whatever it is you've made.

Each of the patterns in this book has specific instructions for finishing when the project requires it. Here is some general advice on how to give your project its well-deserved final touches.

WEAVING IN ENDS

Take the end that needs to be woven in and thread it through a large-eye yarn needle. Working on the wrong side of the piece, weave the yarn in and out along the row for about 2 inches, then turn and weave it in the other direction for a few more stitches, just to lock it in place.

Although it may be a tempting way to save time and effort, never weave in more than one end of yarn at the same place. The doubling up of yarns will create a telltale lump that is sure to show. Also, make certain that your weaving isn't visible on the right side of the work. If you weave in the ends well, they shouldn't show on either side. This is helpful when you are working on a scarf or on anything with the "wrong" side visible. Cut off any excess yarn close to the fabric.

BLOCKING

Blocking is a simple technique that evens out the stitches and smooths any lumpiness in your completed project. If you're making a sweater or other item with multiple pieces, block pieces before sewing them together. Lay out everything on a towel over a flat surface (a bed or table, for instance). Arrange items so they are the exact shape you want, then pin edges in place. For synthetics and blends, mist with water, then allow to dry completely. Lay a damp towel over wools, then hold a steam iron just above the surface, so the steam from the iron and towel penetrates the wool fibers. Take care, however, not to apply pressure or you'll flatten the piece and spoil its texture. After blocking, you'll have a smooth, professional-looking item ready to wear or be sewn together. Most crocheted items can be gently hand washed, but always check the yarn label for specific instructions and temperatures, and lay items flat until dry.

SEWING PIECES TOGETHER

My least favorite part of a project has always been sewing the pieces together. For me, the fun is making the pieces, and the sewing together is just a means to an end. But it does need to be done, and you may find that you *like* sewing the pieces together, so don't let me discourage you.

You'll run into two basic situations when it comes to sewing together a crocheted piece: seaming the side edges and seaming the top or the bottom edges. When you sew sides, you are working with row stitches; when you sew the beginning or ending of a piece, you are working with the tops and bottoms of stitches. Sewing side seams together is a little bit trickier because it's harder to see which loops to take up than when you're working with the familiar top or bottom of stitches. For practice, try sewing together two of your gauge swatches.

To sew vertical edges use matching yarn, thread a large-eyed needle, then carefully match the edges so that the rows align. Weave the yarn in and out of corresponding loops on each piece, as in the illustration.

Sewing vertical edges

When sewing horizontal stitches together (beginning and ending edges), place the two pieces of crocheted fabric together, right sides facing. Take small running stitches just beneath the top loops of the stitches.

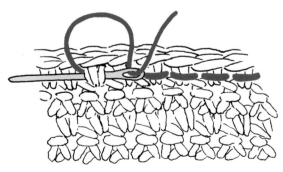

Sewing horizontal tops or bottoms

Anatomy of a Pattern

In order to really understand the ebb and flow of a pattern, with all of the abbreviations and short-hand, I thought it would be a good idea to go through one step-by-step. You don't yet know how to do everything that is in this pattern, but it should help you as you work your way through this book, especially once you're ready to work on a more complex project.

SIZE AND YARN

Indicates the sizes that a project can be made in (usually one size or small, medium, large), and the finished measurements. Yarn information includes type and color as well as quantity.

MATERIALS

All the things you'll need for the project from hook size to extras like beads, sewing materials, buttons, or fabric for a lining.

GAUGE

In this pattern the gauge is measured using a pattern stitch, which means you need to make your gauge swatch in the given pattern stitch and then measure it.

ABBREVIATIONS AND TECHNIQUES

A brief list of what to expect in the pattern, this includes the abbreviations used as well as various techniques like color changing. This is not a standard component of every pattern, but we use it in this book and many beginning patterns have something like it.

PATTERN STITCH

The pattern stitch is the stitch (or stitches) used to create the pattern. Not all projects have a pattern stitch. For instance, if the pattern simply uses plain old single crochet or double crochet, you won't see an explanation of the pattern stitch. Sometimes the pattern stitch includes a color sequence that you must follow.

 Refer to your yarn label for washing and blocking instructions.

bamboo handle purse

SIZES One size
FINISHED MEASUREMENTS 12" x 12"
YARN Cotton Classic by Tahki/Stacy Charles, 100% mercerized cotton, 1.75 oz/50 g (108 yd/100 m) balls
• #3995: 2 skeins

MATERIALS

Hook: Size H/8 (5 mm), *or size needed to obtain gauge*
7" diameter bamboo handle
Large-eye yarn needle
Beads
½ yard matching lining fabric
Sewing thread to match lining
Sewing needle

GAUGE

16 sts = 4" in Pattern Stitch
10 rows = 4" in Pattern Stitch
Take time to make sure your gauge is correct.

ABBREVIATIONS AND TECHNIQUES

Chain	**ch**	(p. 22)
Double crochet	**dc**	(p. 26)
Single crochet	**sc**	(p. 24)
Stitch(es)	**st(s)**	
Triple crochet	**tr**	(p. 30)

PATTERN STITCH

Row 1: Dc in each st, turn.
Row 2: Ch 3 (counts as dc), *skip 1 st, dc in next st, dc in skipped st; repeat from * across row, turn.
Row 3: Ch 1, sc in each st, turn.
Repeat Rows 1–3 for pattern.

THE PURSE (MAKE 2)
To begin: Ch 49; sc in

Working on these sts, and continue until you of the pattern.

HANDLE STITCHES

Row 1: Ch 5, *skip 1 s * across row, ch 5, turn

Row 2: Ch 5, *skip 1 s * across row. End yarn stitch.

FINISHING

Place bag pieces toget Following directions o zontal seams, sew bott

Turn purse right-side follow directions on pa seams to sew side sear seams 4" from top edg

THE PATTERN

This is the body of the pattern with the actual instructions for how to make the project. It begins with how many chain stitches you need to make and then goes on to tell you what stitches, or pattern stitches, to work.

Macramé Fringe

Cut twelve 44" lengths of yarn. Fold each one in half twice to make a piece 11" long. Attach each piece to the bottom of the purse approximately every inch. (Refer to fringe directions on page 45 for attachment techniques.) Follow the illustrated steps below for knotting and adding beads.

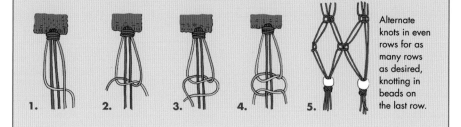

1. 2. 3. 4. 5.

Alternate knots in even rows for as many rows as desired, knotting in beads on the last row.

Measure bag and cut two pieces of lining to match, adding ½" all around for seam allowance.

Place lining pieces together with right sides facing. Taking a ½" seam allowance and starting 4½" from top edge, sew lining together along one side, across bottom, and up the second side, ending 4½" from top edge.

Turn under the top edge and unsewn seam allowances of lining ¼" and then ¼" again to form a hem. Baste. Leave lining wrong-side out.

Slip lining into bag with wrong sides of bag and lining facing each other and top edges aligned. Pin top edge of lining to top edge of bag so that the fold lines up with the last row of bag stitches, just below Row 1 of the handle stitches, and the side edges are even with the side edges of the bag. Use an overcast or blind stitch to sew the lining in place along side seams and top edges.

Place one of the handles under the handle stitches on the wrong side of the bag. Wrap a handle stitch over the handle and pin the stitch to the inside of

the bag. Continue to wrap and pin the handle stitches until all stitches along one top edge are pinned down. Thread yarn through large-eye yarn needle and sew stitches in place where pinned. Repeat on other side.

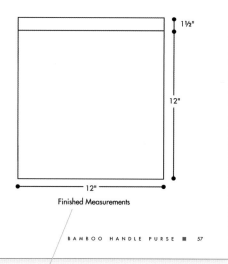

Finished Measurements

(left margin, partial)

8 sc).

ch (at left)
10 repeats

epeat from

epeat from
through last

es facing.
ving hori-
er.

ges aligned,
vertical
ng both

FINISHING

Once you have completed the individual pieces of the project, you need to sew them together and line them if appropriate. Other finishing instructions can include how to make edging or tassels, or how to sew on a fastener or button.

SCHEMATIC

The measurements of each project are given in a visual schematic. If the project is a garment with separate pieces there will be a schematic for each piece.

pick up your
HOOK

For your first project, I want to give you something that is easy enough to complete quickly (so you don't get frustrated) as well as something you'll actually use. These two cases follow the same basic pattern; the eyeglass case is just longer than that for the cell phone. And they are worked in the

cell phone & eyeglass cases

easiest stitch — single crochet. It's fun to try out different yarns and colors. Just remember to check your gauge for each yarn. These make great gifts that you'll be able to do in your sleep once you get the hang of them, so relax and enjoy.

cell phone & eyeglass cases

SIZES One size

FINISHED MEASUREMENTS
- Cell Phone Case: 3½" x 4½"
- Eyeglass Case: 3½" x 6"

YARN Suede by Berroco, 100% nylon, 1.75 oz (50 g)/ 120 yd (111mm) balls
- Wild Bill #3717: 1 ball for Cell Phone Case
- Hopalong Cassidy #3714: 1 ball for Eyeglass Case

MATERIALS

Hook: Size H/8 (5 mm), *or size needed to obtain gauge*
Large-eye yarn needle
1 button for each case

GAUGE

14 sts = 4" in sc
16 rows = 4" in sc
Take time to make sure your gauge is correct.

ABBREVIATIONS AND TECHNIQUES

Chain	**ch**	(p. 22)
Single crochet	**sc**	(p. 24)
Stitch(es)	**st(s)**	

Crocheting the Cell Phone Case

To begin: Chain (ch) 13; single crochet (sc) in second chain (ch) from hook and in each chain (ch) across [12 single crochet (sc)], chain (ch) 1, turn.

Single crochet (sc) in first single crochet (sc) of previous row and in each single crochet (sc) across the row, chain (ch) 1, turn.

Working in this manner, continue until piece measures 10".

Last row: Single crochet (sc) in the first 6 stitches (sts), chain (ch) 3 for the button loop, single crochet (sc) in the last 6 stitches (sts). End yarn by drawing the tail through the last stitch.

FINISHING

With a large-eye yarn needle, weave in any loose ends. Thread the yarn needle with a length of yarn. Fold piece widthwise, leaving 1" at the top edge to serve as a flap. Button loop should be on the flap and the folded-over area should measure about 4½". Following the directions for sewing a vertical seam on page 33, sew the sides of the case. Leave the 1" flap at the top unsewn. Sew button on the front of the case, positioned so that the button loop fastens easily over it when the flap is turned down.

Crocheting the Eyeglass Case

To begin: Chain (ch) 13; single crochet (sc) in second chain (ch) from hook and in each chain (ch) across [12 single crochet (sc)], chain (ch) 1, turn.

Single crochet (sc) in first single crochet (sc) of previous row and in each single crochet (sc) across the row, chain (ch) 1, turn.

Working in this manner, continue until piece measures 13½".

Last row: Single crochet (sc) in the first 6 stitches (sts), chain (ch) 3 for the button loop, single crochet (sc) in the last 6 stitches (sts). End yarn by drawing the tail through the last stitch.

FINISHING

With a large-eye yarn needle, weave in any loose ends. Thread the yarn needle with a length of yarn. Fold piece widthwise, leaving 1" at the top edge to serve as a flap. Button loop should be on the flap and the folded-over area should be about 6". Following the directions for sewing a verticle seam on page 33, sew the sides of the case. Leave the 1" flap at the top unsewn. Sew button on the front of the case, positioned so that the button loop fastens easily over it when the flap is turned down.

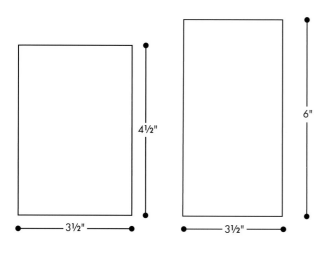

Cell Phone Measurements   Eyeglass Case Measurements

Following the directions for sewing a verticle seam on page 33

The Yarn Label

The packaging on your ball or skein of yarn provides all sorts of handy information. There is some standardization to this information, though yarn from smaller or some European companies may not have all the information that is standard on the labels used by the big American manufacturers. However, most labels provide the length and weight of the yarn in both yards and meters as well as ounces and grams. You can also find information about the fiber content of the yarn — 100% wool; or 70% cotton, 20% silk, 10% Tencel or microfiber; and so on.

Most important, the label should give washing instructions, either in plain English or in universal symbols. It may also refer to suggested gauge and give a suggested hook size for that yarn. Although most yarns give suggested knitting needle sizes, they don't all provide crochet hook sizes. You should make a gauge swatch no matter what, however, so consider whatever advice you find on the label just a starting point.

UNIVERSAL SYMBOLS

gauge recommendations   maximum water temperature

Now that you've gained some confidence, you're ready to try something that uses a few more kinds of stitches. This particular scarf uses three — single crochet, double crochet, and half double crochet — and repeats them to create a pattern stitch. A scarf is perfect to practice your newfound skills with. You won't have any trouble mastering this one, so feel free to make it your own by lengthening or shortening it — a longer length lets you wrap it twice around your neck and still hang enough to look elegant. I've chosen a slightly heavy cotton yarn that will keep you cozy without being too bulky. Cute, retro fringe adds extra length.

basic scarf

basic scarf

SIZES One size

FINISHED MEASUREMENTS 6" x 72"

YARN All Season Cotton by Rowan, 60% cotton/
40% microfiber, 1.75 oz (50 g)/98 yd (90 m) balls
- Limedrop #197: 3 balls

MATERIALS

Hook: Size H/8 (5 mm), *or size needed to obtain gauge*

GAUGE

12 sts = 4" in sc
12 rows = 4" in sc
Take time to make sure your gauge is correct.

ABBREVIATIONS AND TECHNIQUES

Chain	**ch**	(p. 22)
Double crochet	**dc**	(p. 26)
Half double crochet	**hdc**	(p. 28)
Single crochet	**sc**	(p. 24)
Stitch(es)	**st(s)**	

To begin: Ch 19, then sc in second ch from hook and in each ch across (18 sc), ch 2, turn.

Row 1: Hdc in each st across, ch 3, turn.

Row 2: Dc in each st across, ch 1, turn.

Row 3: Sc in each ch across, ch 2, turn.

Repeat Rows 1–3 until piece measures 72". End yarn by drawing tail through the last stitch.

FINISHING

Make and attach fringe as shown on facing page.

Fringe Benefits

You will need 10 fringe, 5 for each end of the scarf. Here's how to make and attach them:

1. For each group of fringe, you will need three 20" lengths of the project yarn. To get even lengths of yarn, cut out a piece of cardboard 8" x 10". Wrap the project yarn around the cardboard 30 times. Cut along one fold line to get 30 pieces of yarn, each 20" long.

2. Make a bundle using three lengths of yarn and fold it in half.

3. Use your crochet hook to draw the folded loop through the edge of the scarf at one end, taking up one row of stitches (See drawing.)

4. With your hook still through the loop, draw the ends through the loop and pull firmly.

5. Attach 5 fringe, evenly spaced across one end of the the scarf. Repeat on the opposite end.

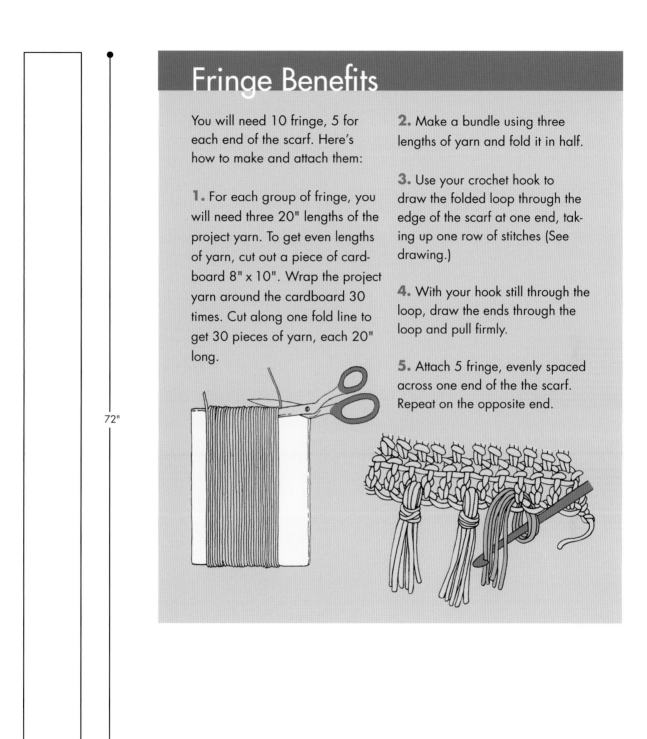

72"

6"

Finished Measurements

Cotton is such a wonderful fiber for a purse — it's sturdy, attractive, and, best of all, washable! And this handbag is as easy to make as it is to take care of. You'll love it not only for its carefree shape, but also for the surprising amount of stuff it holds. It's an attractive, versatile, all-around handbag that is perfectly casual.

swinging ribbon bag

The stitch I use is a variation of the single crochet. It may take a little time to get used to it, but once you've practiced a few rows, it will seem easy. The handle and top edge are trimmed with tri-tone grosgrain ribbon, which keeps it from stretching and adds a fun splash of contrasting color.

swinging ribbon bag

SIZES One size

FINISHED MEASUREMENTS 10" x 11"

YARN Provence by Classic Elite Yarns, 100% mercerized Egyptian cotton, 4⅓ oz (125 g)/256 yd (225 m) skeins
- Ming Blue #2648: 1 skein

MATERIALS

Hook: Size H/8 (5 mm), *or size needed to obtain gauge*
Large-eye yarn needle
1⅔ yards 1-inch grosgrain ribbon

GAUGE

17 sts = 4" in Pattern Stitch
17 rows = 4" in Pattern Stitch
Take time to make sure your gauge is correct.

ABBREVIATIONS AND TECHNIQUES

Chain	**ch**	(p. 22)
Single crochet	**sc**	(p. 24)
Stitch(es)	**st(s)**	

PATTERN STITCH

*Sc in front loop only of next st, then sc in back loop only of next st; repeat from * across, ch 1, turn. Repeat for pattern.

FRONT

To begin: Ch 43; sc in second ch from hook and in each ch across (42 sc), ch 1, turn.

Working on these sts, start Pattern Stitch and continue until you have completed 11".

End yarn by drawing tail through last st.

BACK

Work as for the front.

HANDLES (MAKE 2)

Ch 6; sc in second ch from hook and in each ch across (5 sc), ch 1, turn.

Keeping in sc, work on these sts until piece measures 16". End yarn by drawing tail through last st.

Weave in any loose yarn ends.

With right sides facing each other, place the front and back pieces together.

Following the directions for sewing horizontal seams on page 33, sew the bottom edges together.

Turn the piece so that wrong sides are facing and side edges are aligned.

Follow the directions on page 33 for sewing vertical seams to sew both side seams.

Complete the bag by following the directions for Sewing on the Ribbon in the box below.

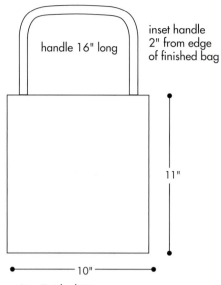

handle 16" long

inset handle 2" from edge of finished bag

11"

10"

Bag Finished Measurements

Sewing on the Ribbon

Measure the top edge of the purse and cut a length of ribbon to match: It should be about 21", including 1" for an overlap. Pin the ribbon along the inside of the bag at the top edge, positioning it so that it begins and ends at one of the side seams.

Use a running stitch to sew ribbon in place, folding under ½" on each end where the ends meet.

Measure the handles and cut two lengths of ribbon to match. They should be about 18" long, including 1" for turning under at each end. Sew ribbons onto one side of each of the purse handles, folding over ½" on each end.

Sew handles to the purse about 2" in from each side seam. Take care not to twist the handles as you position them.

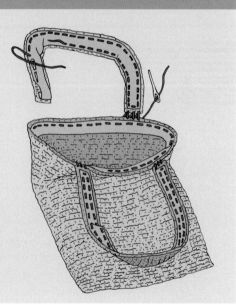

NOW AD

COLOR AND PATTERN

Color is so exciting that once you're able to use it in your crochet projects, you won't want to stop. It's like going from black and white to Technicolor — you're not in Kansas anymore, Dorothy! Master color changing (as well as how to follow a pattern stitch) and you will have the necessary skill and confidence to take on many different projects, not to mention a whole new agenda when it comes to shopping for yarns.

Working with Color

You'll be surprised to discover that you've already learned the basic steps needed for a color change. You simply follow the same method you used for joining a new yarn, but now you're adding an entirely new yarn in a different color rather than continuing with the same yarn.

Sometimes two (or more) colors alternate across a row, as in Fair Isle knitting. Known as "stranding," with this type of color change you crochet with one yarn while carrying the unused yarn loosely across the back of the piece, then switch as specified either in a chart or in a written pattern. It's best to limit your carries to no more than three stitches in length. If you have to carry longer, simply catch up the carried yarn by wrapping the working yarn over it to "tack" it in place.

Another way to change colors is to work with bobbins wound with different colors of yarn. You pick up each one according to the pattern, then wrap the next color around it when you come to it, drop the old one, and continue. The simplest form of color change is the stripe, which allows you to change colors at the end of a row.

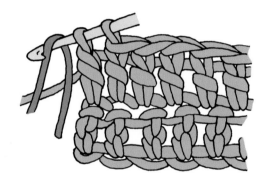

To join a new color yarn, work until you have two loops left on the hook. Draw the new yarn through the two loops to finish the stitch using the new yarn. Leave 6" tails of both yarns to weave into the piece later.

Working Pattern Stitches

Most pattern stitches are simply variations of the basic stitches that you've already learned. The best tip I can give for working on projects with a pattern stitch sequence is to work a practice swatch of the pattern stitch so you won't feel intimidated when you get to the "real thing." When you're working on a new stitch sequence, keep following the directions, even though it doesn't always seem like they will work; in the end, you'll probably be surprised by how well it comes out.

Pattern stitches are a multiple of a certain number of stitches. Some patterns require extra stitches not divisible by the multiple in order to get rows to work out evenly and keep the succeeding rows in sequence. For instance, a pattern may call for 18 stitches, while its multiple is 4. It is said to have a multiple of 4 plus 2. Feels like math class? Don't worry; this will become clearer to you as you get into more difficult stitches.

To experiment, let's look at the pattern stitch used in the Bamboo Handle Purse (page 56). Once you have completed several repeats of the pattern stitch, you should be comfortable enough to do the project. For our practice swatch, chain 21, single crochet in each stitch across, chain 3 more, and then begin the pattern stitch shown in the box.

Sample Pattern Stitch

NOTE: The three drawings below illustrate the steps you need to take in Row 2 of the pattern.

Row 1: Dc in each st, turn.

Row 2: Ch 3 (counts as dc) *skip 1 st, dc in next st, dc in skipped st; repeat from * across row, turn. (See drawings a–c for illustration.)

Row 3: Ch 1, sc in each st, turn.

Repeat Rows 1–3 for pattern.

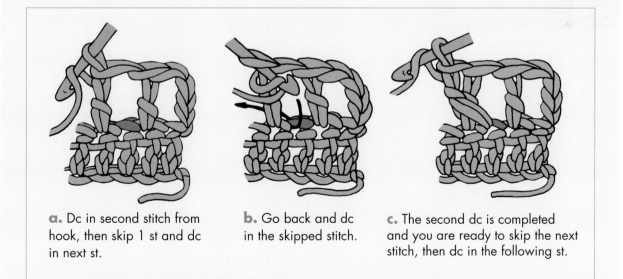

a. Dc in second stitch from hook, then skip 1 st and dc in next st.

b. Go back and dc in the skipped stitch.

c. The second dc is completed and you are ready to skip the next stitch, then dc in the following st.

Now that you're ready to tackle a more complex pattern stitch, this funky purse is an enjoyable project. The knotted fringe with beads and bamboo handle gives it a swinging retro look that you'll love to show off. Handles can be found at any sewing shop or craft supply store in a variety of

bamboo handle purse

materials and sizes. This is a great all-season bag that works in any weather — pair with your favorite sundress and sandals or with boots and a shearling coat. It's both eye-catching and practical, crocheted in a smooth cotton yarn and a rich, sophisticated color that complements any wardrobe.

bamboo handle purse

SIZES One size

FINISHED MEASUREMENTS 12" × 12"

YARN Cotton Classic by Tahki/Stacy Charles, 100% mercerized cotton, 1.75 oz/50 g (108 yd/100 m) balls
- #3995: 2 skeins

MATERIALS

Hook: Size H/8 (5 mm), *or size needed to obtain gauge*
7" diameter bamboo handle
Large-eye yarn needle
Beads
½ yard matching lining fabric
Sewing thread to match lining
Sewing needle

GAUGE

16 sts = 4" in Pattern Stitch
10 rows = 4" in Pattern Stitch
Take time to make sure your gauge is correct.

ABBREVIATIONS AND TECHNIQUES

Chain	**ch**	(p. 22)
Double crochet	**dc**	(p. 26)
Single crochet	**sc**	(p. 24)
Stitch(es)	**st(s)**	
Triple crochet	**tr**	(p. 30)

PATTERN STITCH

Row 1: Dc in each st, turn.
Row 2: Ch 3 (counts as dc), *skip 1 st, dc in next st, dc in skipped st; repeat from * across row, turn.
Row 3: Ch 1, sc in each st, turn.
Repeat Rows 1–3 for pattern.

THE PURSE (MAKE 2)

To begin: Ch 49; sc in each st across (48 sc).

Working on these sts, start Pattern Stitch (at left) and continue until you have completed 10 repeats of the pattern.

HANDLE STITCHES

Row 1: Ch 5, *skip 1 st, tr in next st; repeat from * across row, ch 5, turn.

Row 2: Ch 5, *skip 1 st, tr in next st; repeat from * across row. End yarn by drawing tail through last stitch.

FINISHING

Place bag pieces together with right sides facing. Following directions on page 33 for sewing horizontal seams, sew bottom edges together.

Turn purse right-side out. With side edges aligned, follow directions on page 33 for sewing vertical seams to sew side seams together, ending both seams 4" from top edge.

Macramé Fringe

Cut twelve 44" lengths of yarn. Fold each one in half twice to make a piece 11" long. Attach each piece to the bottom of the purse approximately every inch. (Refer to fringe directions on page 45 for attachment techniques.) Follow the illustrated steps below for knotting and adding beads.

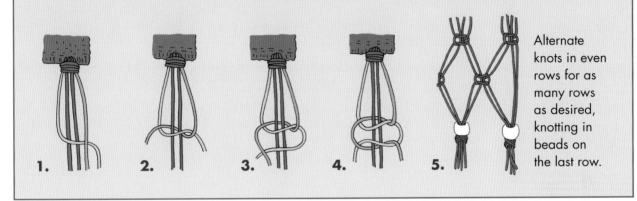

1.   2.   3.   4.   5.

Alternate knots in even rows for as many rows as desired, knotting in beads on the last row.

Measure bag and cut two pieces of lining to match, adding ½" all around for seam allowance.

Place lining pieces together with right sides facing. Taking a ½" seam allowance and starting 4½" from top edge, sew lining together along one side, across bottom, and up the second side, ending 4½" from top edge.

Turn under the top edge and unsewn seam allowances of lining ¼" and then ¼" again to form a hem. Baste. Leave lining wrong-side out.

Slip lining into bag with wrong sides of bag and lining facing each other and top edges aligned. Pin top edge of lining to top edge of bag so that the fold lines up with the last row of bag stitches, just below Row 1 of the handle stitches, and the side edges are even with the side edges of the bag. Use an overcast or blind stitch to sew the lining in place along side seams and top edges.

Place one of the handles under the handle stitches on the wrong side of the bag. Wrap a handle stitch over the handle and pin the stitch to the inside of

the bag. Continue to wrap and pin the handle stitches until all stitches along one top edge are pinned down. Thread yarn through large-eye yarn needle and sew stitches in place where pinned. Repeat on other side.

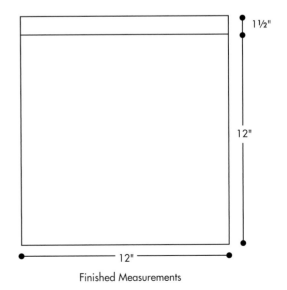

1½"

12"

12"

Finished Measurements

Colorful and warm, a striped scarf is a time-less favorite. This one is completely updated with contemporary colors and a chic long length. Now that you know how to use different colors, it's time to put the skill to use in your own wardrobe! This particular scarf is worked from end to end in vertical stripes. To begin, you work quite a long chain, but the rest of the scarf uses only one stitch, the double crochet, so after the first row it's easy going. There is nothing more thrilling than introducing color to your work, so if you've mastered the basic techniques of crochet, this scarf is an excit-ing, not to mention fashionable, next step.

striped skinny scarf

striped skinny scarf

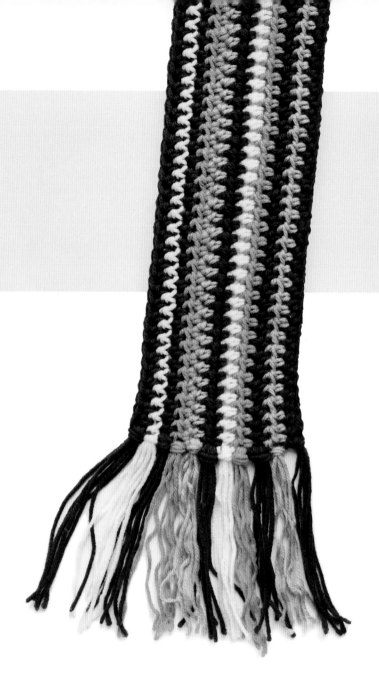

SIZES One size

FINISHED MEASUREMENTS 6" x 90"

YARN Decor by Patons, 75% acrylic/25% wool, 3.5 oz (100 g)/210 yd (192 m) balls

- cc D Rich Aubergine #1627: 1 ball
- cc B Pale Aubergine #1625: 1 ball
- cc A Burgundy #1647: 1 ball
- cc C Pale Olive #1607: 1 ball
- cc E Aran #1602: 1 ball

MATERIALS

Hook: Size I/9 (5.5 mm), *or size needed to obtain gauge*
Large-eye yarn needle

GAUGE

11 sts = 4" in hdc
8 rows = 4" in hdc
Take time to make sure your gauge is correct.

ABBREVIATIONS AND TECHNIQUES

Chain	**ch**	(p. 22)
Changing colors		(p. 52)
Contrasting color	**cc**	
Half double crochet	**hdc**	(p. 28)
Single crochet	**sc**	(p. 24)
Stitch(es)	**st(s)**	

90"

6"

Finished Measurements

Crocheting the Scarf

To begin: With cc A, ch 252; hdc in third ch from hook and in each ch across (250 hdc). In last st, change to cc B and ch 2, turn.

Row 1: With cc B, work 1 hdc in each st to end, change to cc C in last st, ch 2, turn.

Row 2: With cc C, work 1 hdc in each st to end, change to cc D, ch 2, turn.

Row 3: With cc D, work 1 hdc in each st to end, change to cc E in last st, ch 2, turn.

Row 4: With cc E, work 1 hdc in each st to end, change to cc C in last st, ch 2, turn.

Row 5: With cc C, work 1 hdc in each st to end, change to cc B in last st, ch 2, turn.

Row 6: With cc B, work 1 hdc in each st to end, change to cc D in last st, ch 2, turn.

Row 7: With cc D, work 1 hdc in each st to end, change to cc A in last st, ch 2, turn.

Row 8: With cc A, work 1 hdc in each st to end, change to cc E in last st, ch 2, turn.

Row 9: With cc E, work 1 hdc in each st to end, change to cc C in last st, ch 2, turn.

Row 10: With cc C, hdc in each st to end. End yarn.

FINISHING

Weave in all loose ends.

For the fringe, make 22 fringe using three 14" lengths of yarn for each fringe. You will need the following number of fringe: 4 cc A, 4 cc B, 4 cc C, 6 cc D, and 4 cc E. Attach fringe to each end at corresponding colors as shown on page 45.

A Stripe of a Different Color

There are so many wonderful color options, we've included just a few ideas to inspire you. As always, be sure to check your gauge when you switch yarns. Even the same yarn in a different color may require a different-size hook to get the right gauge.

Decorative pillows are a must-have design element that makes any room stylish and comfortable. Knowing how to work with multiple colors will open up new doors for you, and once you're comfortable with the possibilities, suddenly you'll be able to envision a world of color in your home.

striped throw pillow

You needn't be afraid of adding color to a room, and a throw pillow is the perfect way to start. This simple striped pillow, worked in a luscious, rich blend of wool, mohair, and alpaca, is a sumptuous addition to any living space, from a window seat to an easy chair.

striped throw pillow

SIZES One size

FINISHED MEASUREMENTS 14" × 10"

YARN Julia by Goddess Yarns, 50% wool/25% kid mohair/25% alpaca, 1.75 oz (50 g)/93 yd (87 m) balls

- Gold #2163: 1 ball
- Natural #0010: 1 ball
- French Pumpkin #2250: 1 ball
- Rock Henna #2230: 1 ball
- Purple Basil #3158: 1 ball
- Lady's Mantle #3961: 1 ball
- Velvet Moss #6086: 1 ball
- Blue Thyme #4936: 1 ball
- Deep Blue Sea #6396: 1 ball

MATERIALS

Hook: Size H/8 (5 mm), *or size needed to obtain gauge*
Large-eye yarn needle
14" × 10" pillow form

GAUGE

12 sts = 4" in hdc
10 rows = 4" in hdc
Take time to make sure your gauge is correct.

ABBREVIATIONS AND TECHNIQUES

Chain	**ch**	(p. 22)
Changing colors		(p. 52)
Half double crochet	**hdc**	(p. 28)
Stitch(es)	**st(s)**	

To begin: With gold, ch 44; hdc in third ch from hook and in each ch across (42 hdc), ch 2, turn.

Follow color changes shown at right for Stripe Pattern. Continue until you have finished 30 rows.

End yarn.

FINISHING

Weave in all loose ends on wrong side of work.

Assemble pillow as shown in box at right.

Assembling the Pillow

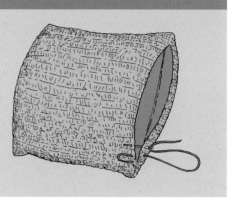

Place pillow pieces together with right sides facing. Following the directions on page 33 for sewing horizontal seams, sew the two long sides and one end together. Sew together the other end about 2" in from each side edge, leaving an opening to insert the pillow form. Insert the pillow form, pushing it in at each corner to fill out the spaces. Follow the directions on page 33 for sewing vertical seams to finish the opening.

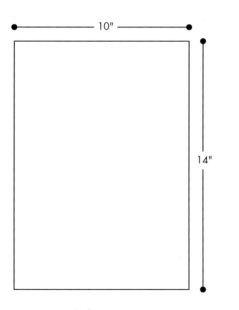

Finished Measurements

STRIPE PILLOW COLOR PATTERN

Rows 1 & 2: Gold

Row 3: Natural

Rows 4 & 5: French Pumpkin

Rows 6 & 7: Rock Henna

Rows 8 & 9: Purple Basil

Row 10: Lady's Mantle

Rows 11 & 12: Velvet Moss

Rows 13 & 14: Blue Thyme

Rows 15 & 16: Deep Blue Sea

Rows 17 & 18: Blue Thyme

Rows 19 & 20: Velvet Moss

Row 21: Lady's Mantle

Rows 22 & 23: Purple Basil

Rows 24 & 25: Rock Henna

Rows 26 & 27: French Pumpkin

Row 28: Natural

Rows 29 & 30: Gold

SHAPING

SHAPING AND FITTING

Knowing how to shape a crocheted piece allows you to make stuff that you can wear. To create shape, you simply increase or decrease a stitch. To make an armhole, for instance, your pattern will tell you to decrease a certain number of stitches. To make a sleeve, you add stitches as instructed. And sometimes you need to slip a stitch so that you can move across a row without adding any height.

Decrease (dec)

To decrease, you can either stop short of finishing a row, slip stitch (see facing page) across a given number of stitches to take them out of use (see at right), or, most common, work two stitches together (referred to as "dec" in pattern). The following illustrations show how to work two stitches together.

1. In single crochet, insert hook through next two stitches. Yarn over once, then draw yarn through all loops on hook.

2. When decrease is complete, you have one loop on hook.

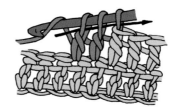

1. In double crochet, work a double crochet stitch until you have two loops on hook. Keep these two loops on hook and begin a double crochet in next stitch.

2. Work the double crochet stitch until you have three loops on hook. Yarn over once, then draw yarn through all three loops.

3. When decrease is complete, you have one loop on hook.

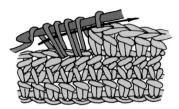

1. In half double crochet, begin a half double crochet (yarn over, insert hook through next stitch, yarn over, and draw yarn through). With three loops on hook, begin next half double crochet (yarn over, insert hook through next stitch, and draw yarn through). Yarn over and draw yarn through all five loops on hook.

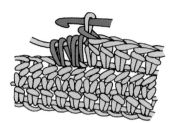

2. When decrease is complete, you have one loop on hook.

1. In triple crochet, work a triple crochet until you have two loops on hook. Yarn over twice and insert hook into next stitch in row.

2. Begin a triple crochet in next stitch. Continue to work triple crochet, drawing yarn through two loops at a time until you have three stitches on hook, then draw yarn through all three stitches to complete decrease with one stitch left on hook.

Increase (inc)

To increase, work two stitches in the same space. You can do this when you're working any type of stitch, from single to triple crochet.

Slip Stitch (sl st)

The **slip stitch** is a way of joining or moving across a stitch without adding height or another stitch.

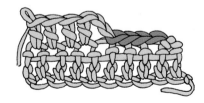

1. Insert hook into top loop of stitch and draw yarn through both top loop of stitch and loop on hook without any yarn overs.

2. Here, the first three stitches at the right are slip stitches, allowing you to move from the edge to the fifth stitch without adding height.

A perennial favorite with a sexy twist, this wrap is crocheted with merino combined with a yarn that has a subtle sparkle, making it the perfect cover-up for an elegant evening dress — or just throw it on over jeans! This shawl is not only cozy, but also sleek, sophisticated. You probably don't think of a shawl as the most shapely item in your closet, but it's actually the perfect garment for trying out your new shaping skills. It's worked with a large hook for a fabulous cobweb effect. The large hook also makes the work go fast, so you'll easily finish it in time for your next party. See Yarn Options on page 73 for other possibilities.

the little black wrap

the little black wrap

SIZES One size

FINISHED MEASUREMENTS
- Top width: 50"
- Length: 36"

YARNS

Madelaine by Knit One Crochet Too, 100% superfine merino wool, 1.75 oz (50 g)/198 yd (181 m) hanks
- Jet #900: 3 hanks

Sprinkles by Knit One Crochet Too, 60% polyamide/40% viscose, 1.75 oz (50 g)/190 yd (174 m) hanks
- Jet #900: 3 hanks

MATERIALS

Hook: Size I/9 (5.5 mm), *or size needed to obtain gauge*

Large-eye yarn needle

GAUGE

12 sts = 4" in dc with one strand of each yarn held together

10 rows = 4" in dc with one strand of each yarn held together

Take time to make sure your gauge is correct.

ABBREVIATIONS AND TECHNIQUES

Chain	**ch**	(p. 22)
Decrease	**dec**	(p. 68)
Double crochet	**dc**	(p. 26)
Fringe		(p. 45)
Stitch(es)	**st(s)**	

PATTERN STITCH

Row 1: *Ch 1, skip 1 st, dc in next st; repeat from * across row.

Row 1: Holding 1 strand of each yarn together, ch 152; dc in fourth ch from hook and in each ch across (149 dc), ch 4, turn.

Row 2: Dc in third st, begin Pattern Stitch, ch 4, turn. (The beginning ch 4 on each row counts as a dc and a ch 1.)

Row 3: Dc in third st, follow Pattern Stitch across until you reach the last dc right before the ch 4 turning ch, dec in the last 2 sts, ch 4, turn.

Next Rows: Repeat Row 3, decreasing in the third st at the beginning and 1 in the last 2 sts of every row until you have 2 dc left.

End yarn by drawing tail through the last stitch.

FINISHING

You will need 27 fringe. For each fringe, cut two 36" lengths of project yarn. Fold the pair of yarns in half twice to create a bundle of yarn with 8 strands about 9" long.

Attach one fringe at each corner of the shawl, then attach the remaining fringe evenly spaced along each side, 12 fringe to each side. (See page 45 for illustration of how to make and attach the fringe.)

Yarn Options

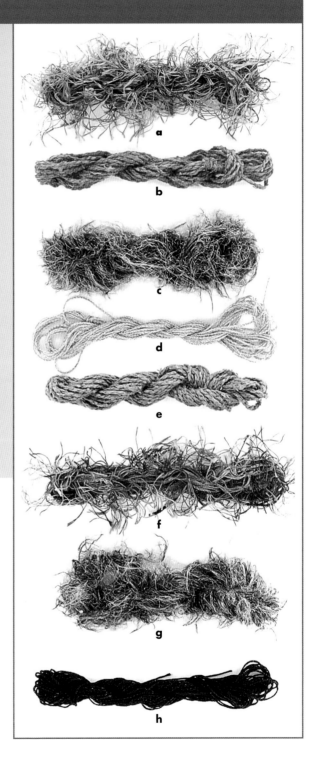

a Plume FX by Berroco, 100% polyester, .70 oz (20 g)/63 yd (58 m) balls, #6862

b Summer Tweed by Rowan, 70% silk/30% cotton, 50 g/118 yd (108 m) balls, #SH509

c Glitz by Berroco, 100% nylon, .875 oz (25 g)/70 yd (65 m) balls, #9711

d Lurex Shimmer by Rowan, 80% viscose/20% polyester, 25 g/104 yd (95 m) balls, #SH332 (use with c)

e Summer Tweed by Rowan, 70% silk/30% cotton, 50 g/118 yd (108 m) balls, #SH10

f Plume FX by Berroco, 100% polyester, .70 oz (20 g)/63 yd (58 m) balls, #6822

g Glitz by Berroco, 100% nylon, .875 oz (25 g)/70 yd (65 m), #9702

h Lurex Shimmer by Rowan, 80% viscose/20% polyester, 25 g/104 yd (95 m) balls, #SH334 (use with g)

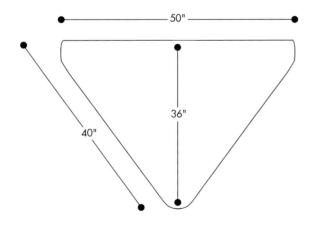

Finished Measurements

Graceful and feminine, this lacy little top with its square neckline and flirty bodice is sure to flatter. With several different pattern stitches as well as shaping techniques involved, plan to take your time with this project. I've chosen a soft cotton yarn with a wonderful drape that will show off

lacy sleeveless shell

any figure, whether you wear it over a camisole of a contrasting color or over your cutest bikini top. I like small, elegant mother-of-pearl buttons, but you can change the look with leather or natural horn buttons. For a truly accomplished look, pay attention to the finishing on this project.

lacy sleeveless shell

SIZES	SMALL	MEDIUM	LARGE
ACTUAL CHEST MEASUREMENT	32"	35"	38"
FINISHED CHEST MEASUREMENT	34"	37"	40"
FINISHED LENGTH	18"	20½"	23"
YARN 4-Ply Cotton by Rowan, 100% cotton, 1.75 oz (50 g)/ 184 yd (170 m) balls			
• White #726	6 balls	7 balls	8 balls

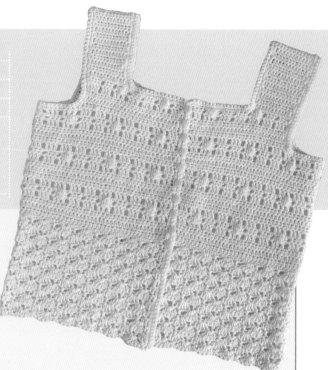

MATERIALS

Hook: Size F/5 (3.75 mm), *or size needed to obtain gauge*
Large-eye yarn needle
10 small buttons

GAUGE

18 hdc = 4"
2 repeats of Bodice Pattern Stitch = 3"
Take time to make sure your gauge is correct.

ABBREVIATIONS AND TECHNIQUES

Bobble Stitch		(below)
Chain	**ch**	(p. 22)
Double crochet	**dc**	(p. 26)
Half double crochet	**hdc**	(p. 28)
Single crochet	**sc**	(p. 24)
Slip Stitch	**sl st**	(p. 69)
Stitch(es)	**st(s)**	
Yarn over	**yo**	(p. 18)

PATTERN STITCHES

Bobble Stitch

Row 1: *Yo, draw up a loop, yo, draw through 2 loops on hook; repeat from * 3 more times, yo, draw through all 5 loops on hook.

Bodice Pattern Stitch (multiple of 4 + 3 sts)

Rows 1–3: Hdc across row.
Row 4: 3 dc, *ch 1, skip 1 st, 1 dc in next 3 sts; repeat from * across row.
Row 5: Hdc in 3 sts, *ch 1, skip next ch 1 space, hdc in next st, Bobble Stitch in next st, hdc in next st, ch 1, hdc in 3 sts, ch 1, skip ch, hdc in 3 sts; repeat from * across row.
Row 6: Repeat Row 4.

Shell Pattern Stitch (multiple of 6 + 3)

Row 1: Hdc, *skip 2 sts, 5 dc in next st, skip 2 sts, hdc in next st; repeat from * across row, ch 3, turn.
Row 2: 2 dc in ch 3 space, *hdc in middle dc of 5 dc, 5 dc in hdc; repeat from * across row, ending 3 dc in last hdc.
Row 3: Ch 3, *5 dc in hdc, hdc in middle dc of 5 dc; repeat from * across row, ending with a hdc. Repeat Rows 2 and 3 for pattern.

BODICE

To begin: Ch **157** (**169**, **181**); work hdc in third ch from hook and in each ch across [**155** (**167**, **179**) hdc].

Row 2: Work Row 2 of Bodice Pattern Stitch.

Next Rows: Continue in Bodice Pattern Stitch until piece measures **6** (**7**, **8**) inches.

NOTE: Bodice is worked in one piece. Complete a pattern sequence and end ready for a wrong-side row.

LEFT FRONT OF BODICE

Work across **28** (**30**, **32**) sts, making sure to maintain Bodice Pattern Stitch as established on back. (Leave remaining sts unworked.)

Work on just these sts for **1½** (**2**, **2½**) inches. End yarn, ready for a right-side row.

LEFT STRAP

Hdc in 12 sts. (Leave remaining sts unworked.)

Work in hdc for **9** (**10**, **11**) inches; end yarn.

BACK

With wrong side facing, skip **21** (**23**, **25**) sts from last st on Left Front; join yarn and work in Bodice Pattern Stitch across **57** (**61**, **65**) sts. (Leave remaining sts unworked.) Turn. Work even in pattern for 2". End yarn.

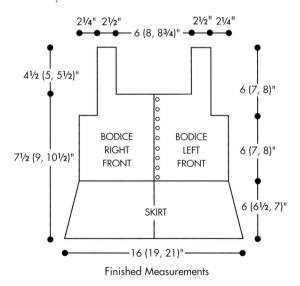

2¼" 2½"   2½" 2¼"

6 (8, 8¾)"

4½ (5, 5½)"

6 (7, 8)"

7½ (9, 10½)"

BODICE RIGHT FRONT   BODICE LEFT FRONT

6 (7, 8)"

SKIRT

6 (6½, 7)"

16 (19, 21)"

Finished Measurements

RIGHT FRONT OF BODICE

With wrong side facing, skip **21** (**23**, **25**) sts from last st of back, attach yarn, and work in established pattern across remaining **28** (**30**, **32**) sts. Work even for **1½** (**2**, **2½**) inches, ending ready for a right-side row. End yarn.

RIGHT STRAP

Skip **16** (**18**, **20**) sts.

Join yarn on **17th** (**19th**, **21st**) st.

Ch 2, hdc in same st and in remaining 11 sts. Work even in hdc on 12 sts for **9** (**10**, **11**) inches. End yarn.

BODICE SKIRT

With right side facing, sc around bottom of bodice, working in remaining loop of beginning ch and making any necessary adjustments to have **159** (**171**, **183**) sts. Begin Row 1 of Shell Pattern Stitch and work even in this pattern stitch until skirt measures **6** (**6½**, **7**) inches from bottom of bodice.

FINISHING

Using project yarn and large-eye yarn needle, sew straps to back of bodice.

With right side facing, attach yarn at any underarm st. Sc evenly around armhole to begin, sl st to join; turn. Sc in each sc around, sl st to join. End yarn.

BUTTON BAND

With right side facing, attach yarn at lower edge of right side of skirt. Sc evenly up right side, around neck, and down left side, working 3 sc in each corner. Turn.

Mark right side of bodice for 10 buttonholes, with top button at neck edge and bottom button at bottom of bodice. (Leave skirt free.)

Sc up left front and around neck. *Sc in each sc to mark for buttonhole, ch 1, skip 1; repeat from * to beginning of skirt. Sc in each sc to bottom of skirt. End yarn.

Sew buttons opposite buttonholes.

The delightful bold stripes in this adorable sweater are sure to win over the little tot in your life. This project uses techniques that you have already learned — following a pattern stitch, color changing, and some shaping. Baby clothes are great first-time projects. Because they're so small, you're

candy stripe baby sweater

finished before you have a chance to tire of them. The soft cotton/wool blend that I've chosen for this sweater is perfect for sensitive skin. A handmade gift is always cherished, so crochet with care and this will be something truly special to bestow.

candy stripe baby sweater

SIZES	SMALL (6 MO)	MEDIUM (12 MO)	LARGE (18 MO)
FINISHED CHEST MEASUREMENTS	20"	22"	24"
FINISHED LENGTH	10"	11"	12"

YARN Wool cotton/Rowan 50% merino wool/50% cotton, 1.75 oz (50g)/123 yd (113m) balls

• cc A Citron #901	1 ball	1 ball	1 ball
• cc B Aqua #949	2 balls	2 balls	2 balls
• cc C Antique #900	2 balls	2 balls	2 balls
• cc D August #953	2 balls	2 balls	2 balls

MATERIALS

Hook: Size G/6 (4 mm), *or size needed to obtain gauge*

Large-eye yarn needle

Five ¾" buttons

GAUGE

16 sts = 4", 16 rows = 4" in Pattern Stitch
Take time to make sure your gauge is correct.

ABBREVIATIONS AND TECHNIQUES

Chain	ch	(p. 22)
Contrasting color	cc	
Decrease	dec	(p. 68)
Single crochet	sc	(p. 24)
Stitch(es)	st(s)	

PATTERN STITCH

*Sc in the next st in the front loop only, sc in the next st in the back loop only; repeat from * across row, ch 1, turn. Repeat this row for pattern.

STRIPE SEQUENCE

Row 1: (Aqua)
Row 2: (Antique)
Row 3: (August)

BACK

To begin: With cc A, ch **41** (**45**, **49**); work sc in second ch from hook and in each ch across [**40** (**44**, **48**) sc]. Change to cc B in last st, ch 2, turn.

Working on these sts, begin Pattern Stitch. As you work the pattern, change colors each row, maintaining this striping sequence: cc B, cc C, cc D.

Work even until piece measures **10** (**11**, **12**) inches. End yarn.

LEFT FRONT

To begin: With Citron, ch **19** (**21**, **23**); work sc in second ch from hook and in each ch across [**18** (**20**, **22**) sc], changing to cc B in last st, ch 2, turn.

Working on these sts, begin Pattern Stitch. Be sure to follow same stripe color sequence used on back.

Work even in Pattern Stitch until piece measures **6½** (**7**, **7½**) inches; end ready for a right-side row.

Neck shaping: Keeping in Pattern Stitch and striping, dec 1 st every other row at neck edge **6** (**8**, **8**) times. You will have **12** (**12**, **14**) sts. Work even in Pattern Stitch until piece is same length (and with same number of stripes) as on back.

RIGHT FRONT

Work as for Left Front, but reverse the shaping. **Note:** End ready for a wrong-side row to reverse neck shaping.

SLEEVES (MAKE 2)

To begin: With cc A, ch **25** (**27**, **29**); work sc in second ch from hook and in each ch across [**24** (**26**, **28**) sc], changing to cc B in last st, ch 2, turn.

Working on these sts, follow Pattern Stitch and stripe sequence as before. At the same time, include 1 st each side every 4 rows **6** (**7**, **8**) times. You will have **36** (**40**, **44**) sts.

Work even in Pattern Stitch until piece measures **7** (**8**, **9**) inches. End yarn.

POCKETS (MAKE 2)

With cc A, ch 11; work sc in second ch from hook and in each ch across (10 sc), ch 2, turn. Continue working these sts in sc until you have completed 11 rows. End yarn.

BUTTON BAND

To begin: Mark left side of sweater for 5 buttons, with the bottom button at lower edge of sweater, the top button at beginning of neck shaping, and remaining buttons evenly spaced in between.

Row 1: With right side facing, attach yarn at bottom edge of right-hand side of sweater. Sc evenly up right front, around neck, and down left front, working 2 sc at beginning and end of neck shaping and working 2 sts together to dec at shoulder seams. Ch 1, turn. **Note:** Count sts on right front and left front to make certain you have the same number of sts on each front.

Row 2 (buttonhole row): On the wrong side, *sc to marker, ch 1, skip 1 st; repeat from * to neck shaping, then sc in each sc to bottom of right front, working 2 sc at beginning and end of neck shaping and working 2 sts together at shoulder seams. Ch 1, turn.

Row 3: Sc in each sc and ch space up the right front, around neck, and down left front. End yarn.

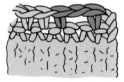

working a buttonhole

FINISHING

Mark the middle of the top sleeve edge. Pin the sleeve to the armhole edge, with wrong sides facing and center of sleeve at shoulder. Follow instructions for sewing horizontal seams on page 33 to stitch sleeve of sweater.

Use the same stitch to sew sleeve and side seams, taking care to match pieces at bottom edges and at the underarm. Repeat for other sleeve.

Pin pockets in place, positioned so that bottom edge of sweater and side edges of pockets are 6 stitches in from side seams.

Sew buttons to button band, positioning them opposite correlating buttonholes.

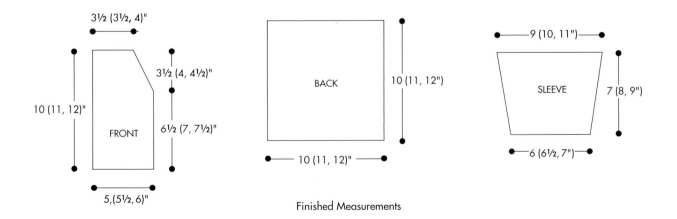

Finished Measurements

If you ever wanted to prance around the cabana in high heels, this would be the bikini to do it in. Crocheted in a sleek mercerized cotton that gives it a subtle sheen, this teeny tiny sweetheart of a suit may not be exactly why you learned to crochet in the first place, but it's a spectacular excuse

the swimsuit issue bikini

to put your hook to work. The triangular cups have just the right amount of shaping. The traditional ties are a cinch to do and make this the sassiest suit on the beach. It's really suitable only for serious sunbathing, so don't plan on rolling around in rough surf in this fashionable garment!

the swimsuit issue bikini

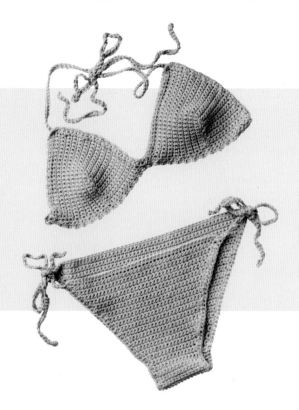

SIZES	SMALL/MED	MED/LARGE
FINISHED MEASUREMENTS		
•Bra top (cup size)	A/B	B/C
•Bottom front	8"	9½"
•Bottom back	11"	14"
YARN Grace by Patons, 100% mercerized cotton, 1.75 oz (50 g)/136 yd (125 m) balls		
•Light blue #60130	2 balls	2 balls

MATERIALS

Hook: Size F/5 (3.75 mm), *or size needed to obtain gauge*
Large-eye yarn needle

GAUGE

18 sts = 4" in sc
24 rows = 4" in sc
Take time to make sure your gauge is correct.

ABBREVIATIONS AND TECHNIQUES

Chain	**ch**	(p. 22)
Decrease	**dec**	(p. 68)
Half double crochet	**hdc**	(p. 28)
Increase	**inc**	(p. 69)
Single crochet	**sc**	(p. 24)
Slip stitch	**slp st**	(p. 69)
Stitch(es)	**st(s)**	

BRA (MAKE 2)

To begin: Ch **25** (**33**); sc in second ch from hook and in each ch across [**24** (**32**) sts], ch 1, turn.

Working in sc on these sts, work for **16** (**20**) rows, ch 1, turn.

Keeping in sc, work across **12** (**16**) sts, ch 1, turn.

Work on these sts for **13** (**17**) rows. End yarn.

Note: Cotton yarn becomes very stretchy when wet. Wear with care!

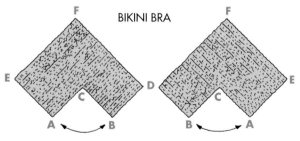

BIKINI BRA

FINISHING THE BRA

To complete cup shaping, pin edges AC and BC together and stitch, following directions for vertical seams on page 33. Use project yarn to tack the two cups together at D.

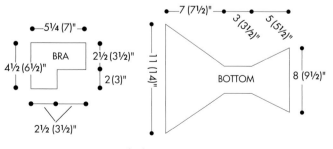

Finished Measurements

For back tie, ch 101; sc in second ch from hook and each ch across.

Starting at E, sc in each sc and each row, ch **2** (**4**) at D, then sc in each sc and row to the other E.

Without breaking yarn, ch 101, sc in second ch from hook and in each ch across for back tie. You are now back at E.

Work sc in each st to F. For neck tie, ch 101, sc in second ch from hook and each ch across, sl st to st where you began at F.

Continue working sc in each row to D. In this ch **2** (**4**) space, sc in each ch, then continue up other side of bra to F. Do not end yarn.

For second neck tie, ch 101, sc in second ch from hook and each ch across for necktie, then sl st to beginning st at F.

Continue working sc in each st to E. For second back tie, ch 101, sc in second ch from hook and in each ch across to beginning ch at E. Ch 1, turn.

On the wrong side, *sc, ch 2, skip 1 st; repeat from * around entire bra top, working a sl st behind back and neck ties.

Join with sl st to first sc. End yarn.

BOTTOM

To begin: Ch **37** (**45**); sc in second ch from hook and each ch across [**36** (**44**) sts], ch 1, turn.

Work one more row even.

Continuing in sc, dec 1 st each side every other row **6** (**8**) times [**24** (**28**) sts], then dec 1 st each side every 3 rows 6 times [**12** (**16**) sts].

Work even on these st for **3** (**3½**) inches.

Continuing in sc, inc 1 st each side every other row **19** (**23**) times [**50** (**62**) sts]. End yarn.

FINISHING THE BOTTOM

To begin: For front tie, ch 51; sc in second ch from hook and each ch across.

BIKINI BOTTOM

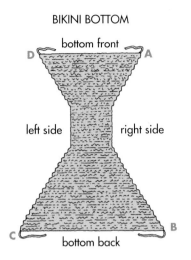

Beginning at A, hdc in each st across. For tie, ch 51; sc in second ch from hook and each ch across.

Working up side of left front, *hdc in each of next 4 sts, then work next 2 sts together (dec); repeat from * until you reach B at top of back.

For back tie, ch 51, sc in second ch from hook and in each ch across. (You are back at B.)

Working across top of back, sc in each st to C. Ch 51; sc in second ch from hook and each ch across for other back tie.

Working down right side of back, *hdc in each of next 4 stitches, then work next 2 sts together (dec); repeat from * to D.

For second front tie, ch 51; sc in second ch from hook and each ch across until you are back at D.

Work across top of front in sc to first hdc at A. Join with sl st to first hdc. End yarn.

FLOWER

Ch 4; join with a sl st to form a circle. (Sc, ch 3) into circle 5 times ending with sc. End yarn, leaving a 6" tail.

Use tail threaded through a large-eye needle to sew flower onto center of bra top.

not your
GRANNY

GRANNIES AND POSIES

Granny squares, or "motifs," as they are sometimes referred to, are used in a variety of ways. Probably the most memorable is the ubiquitous granny square afghan. Although personally I love these afghans because they are retro and fun, it just so happens that there are dozens of other things you can do with this simple square, including pretty little flowers (which follow the same basic technique and so are really not that far from grannies on the crochet timeline). The biggest challenge to working with granny squares is the time it takes to sew them all together. But if you make it into a sort of Zen-like experience and just go with the flow, the effort pays off in the end.

Working with Circles

The basis for a huge family of crochet projects is a circle, created by slip stitching a number of chain stitches together. Adding this technique to your crochet repertoire opens the door to all kinds of fun projects, including granny squares and flowers. Since both begin with a circle, once you master the circle you can create these and many other shapes with any stitch — single crochet, double crochet, and so on — worked into that circle.

To work double crochet in a 4-chain circle, chain 3 (turning chain), turn, then work 5 double crochet into the circle. (Insert the hook into the circle itself, not into chain stitches that form the circle.)

To join stitches into a circle, chain 4, then insert hook into first chain, yarn over, and draw yarn through chain and loop on hook with no further yarn overs.

To join circle, insert hook into top chain of turning ch 3, yarn over, then draw yarn through top chain and loop on hook with no further yarn overs.

Basic Granny Square

Let's practice by making the most basic type of granny square. Once you have mastered this, you'll be ready to try all kinds of variations and make cool stuff, from handbags and afghans, to potholders or you name it. Grannies are easy to get hooked on, because not only are they incredibly easy, but they're also extremely portable and a great way to show off lots of color. Examine the square at the right and imagine what it would look like if every round were crocheted in a different color. (For an opportunity to explore color changes in granny squares, see Red-Hot Granny Scarf, page 98.)

For this practice square, you should use a size H/8 (5 mm) hook and about 5 yards each of four different colors of scrap yarn. Try to use yarn that's all the same weight; a worsted weight is easiest to work with.

To begin: Ch 4, then join the last ch with a sl st to the first ch to form a ring.

Rnd 1 (right side): Ch 3 (counts as 1 dc), work 2 dc into ring, ch 2, *work 3 dc into ring, ch 2; repeat from * 2 more times. Join round with a sl st in 3rd ch of ch 3. Fasten off. From wrong side, join next color with a sl st in any ch 2 space.

Rnd 2: Ch 3, work 2 dc in same ch 2 sp, ch 1, *work (3 dc, ch 2, 3 dc) in next ch 2 space, ch 1; rep from * 2 more times, end with 3 dc in beginning ch 2 space, ch 2, join round with a sl st in third ch of ch 3. Fasten off. From right side, join next color with a sl st in any ch 2 space.

Rnd 3: Ch 3, work 2 dc in same ch 2 space, ch 1, *work 3 dc in next ch 1 space, ch 1, work (3 dc, ch 2, 3 dc) in next ch 2 sp, ch 1; repeat from * 2 more times, end with 3 dc in next ch 1 space, ch 1, 3 dc in beginning ch 2 space, ch 2. Join round with a sl st in third ch of ch 3. Fasten off. From wrong side, join next color with a sl st in any ch 2 space.

Rnd 4: Ch 3, work 2 dc in same ch 2 space, ch 1 *(work 3 dc in next ch 1 space, ch 1) twice, work (3 dc, ch 2, 3 dc) in next ch 2 space, ch 1; repeat from * 2 more times, end with (work 3 dc in next ch 1 sp, ch 1) twice, 3 dc in beginning ch 2 sp, ch 2. Join round with a sl st in 3rd ch of ch 3. End by cutting yarn and drawing the tail through the last loop. Weave in all loose ends.

Round 1   Round 2   Round 3   Round 4

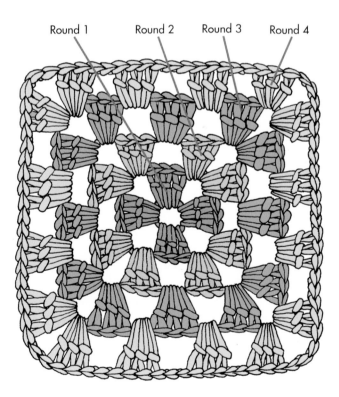

Basic Granny Square

Basic Flower

The flower motif is started in exactly the same manner as the granny. Flowers are just as easy to make and you can use them in many different ways. For these two practice flowers, use a worsted-weight yarn and a size H/8 (5 mm) hook. As you work them, you'll discover that you're creating three-dimensional flowers, each with two layers of "petals."

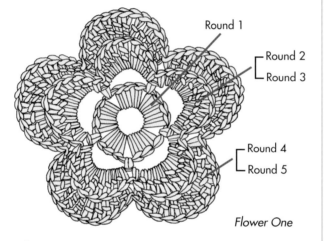

Flower One

Flower One

Note: Rnds 2 and 4 are difficult to identify in the drawing, as they form the structure on which to crochet Rounds 3 and 5.

To begin: Ch 5, join with a sl st to first ch to form ring.

Rnd 1: Ch 2 (counts as 1 sc), work 15 sc into ring, join with sl st to beginning ch.

Rnd 2: °Ch 4, skip 2 sc, sl st in next sc; repeat from ° 4 more times, ending last st in base of beginning ch.

Rnd 3: In each ch 4 sp around work, (1 sc, 4 dc, 1 tr, 4 dc, 1 sc); join with sl st to first sc.

Rnd 4: °Ch 5, sl st between next 2 sc (between petals); repeat from ° 4 more times, ending with a sl st to base of beginning ch.

Rnd 5: In each ch 5 space, ch 1, work (1 sc, 5 dc, 3 tr, 5 dc, 1 sc) around, ending with a sl st to beginning ch. End yarn, leaving a long tail of at least 6".

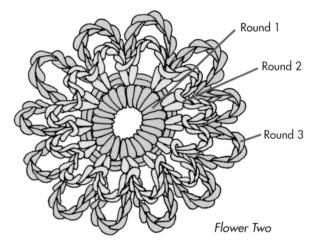

Flower Two

Flower Two

To begin: Ch 4, join with sl st to first ch to form ring.

Rnd 1: Ch 2 (counts as 1 sc), work 11 sc into ring, join with sl st to beginning ch (12 sc, including the ch 2).

Rnd 2: Working in front loop only, work 1 sc, 4 ch, 1 sc into each sc around.

Rnd 3: Working into the back half only of each sc of Rnd 1, work 1 sc, ch 6, 1 sc into each sc. End yarn, leaving a long tail of at least 6".

flower pin

YARN Star by Classic Elite Yarns, 99% cotton/1% Lycra

4 oz (50 g)/112 yd (102 m) skeins
- Natural #5116: 1 skein
- #5132: 5 yd

MATERIALS

Hook: Size I/9 (5.5 mm), *or size needed to obtain gauge*
Large-eye yarn needle
6 square inches of white felt
1" pin back

GAUGE

14 sts = 4", 15 rows = 4"

Note: Even though you aren't creating a flat piece of fabric, you may want to work a 6"- square gauge swatch to ensure the right-size flowers. The finished pin should be about 3½" across.

ABBREVIATIONS AND TECHNIQUES

Chain	**ch**	(p. 22)
Single crochet	**sc**	(p. 24)
Slip stitch	**sl st**	(p. 69)
Yarn over	**yo**	(p. 18)

FLOWER

To begin: Ch 4. Join with a sl st to first ch to form ring.

Rnd 1: Ch 2 (counts as 1 sc), work 11 sc into ring, then join with sl st to beginning ch, 12 sc including the ch 2.

Rnd 2: Working in front loop only of each sc, work (*1 sc, 4 ch, 1 sc*) into each sc.

Rnd 3: Working into the back half only of each sc of Rnd 1, *1 sc, ch 6, 1 sc; in the next sc work 1 sc, ch 4, 1 sc; repeat from * to end.

End yarn and leave a long tail of at least 6".

FLOWER CENTER

Ch 3, *yo, insert hook into first ch, and pull through 2 loops; repeat from * 4 more times.

Yo, pull through all 6 loops on hook.

Cut yarn, leaving a long tail of at least 6", and pull through last loop.

FINISHING

With white yarn, make flower as above and make center with pink yarn.

Sew center into center of flower with long tail and weave in ends.

With white felt, make a circle about 1½" across and sew onto the back of the flower.

Sew pin-back onto felt.

Oh, the versatile little flower! You won't believe how easy these are, or how much fun you can have putting them on things. Don't be afraid to experiment with these handmade blossoms. In the right colors and yarns, they're playful, girlish additions to any tank top or camisole. You'll find endless uses for them as charming elements on denim jackets and knit handbags or as a pretty topping for a vintage sweater collar. Sew them into a length of ribbon to create a lovely sash. Master this simple technique and enjoy all the hidden possibilities it has to offer.

posies for tanks

posies for tanks

SIZE One size

YARN Grace by Patons, 100% mercerized cotton,
1.75 oz (50 g)/136 yd (125 m) balls

　Blush #60416: 1 ball
　Viola #60322: 1 ball
　Fern #60527: 1 ball

Cotton Classic by Tahki, 100% mercerized cotton,
1.75 oz (50 g)/108 yd (100 m) skeins

　Yellow #3532: 1 skein

MATERIALS

Hook: Size G/6 (4 mm), *or size needed to obtain gauge*

Sharp large-eye yarn needle and matching sewing thread

T-shirt or tank top of your choice

GAUGE

18 sts = 4" in sc using Grace
24 rows = 4" in sc using Grace

16 sts = 4" in sc using Cotton Classic
20 rows = 4" in sc using Cotton Classic

Note: Even though you aren't creating a flat piece of fabric, you may want to work a 6"- square gauge swatch to ensure the right-size flowers.

ABBREVIATIONS AND TECHNIQUES

Chain	ch	(p. 22)
Crocheted flower		(p. 90)
Double crochet	dc	(p. 26)
Half double crochet	hdc	(p. 28)
Single crochet	sc	(p. 24)
Slip stitch	sl st	(p. 69)
Triple crochet	tr	(p. 30)
Yarn over	yo	(p. 18)

Crocheting the Flowers and Leaves

LARGE FLAT FLOWER

To begin: Ch 5; join with a sl st to first ch to form ring.

Rnd 1: Ch 2 (counts as 1 sc), work 15 sc into ring, then join with sl st to beginning ch (16 sc including the ch 2).

Rnd 2: *Ch 4, skip 2 sc, sl st in next sc; repeat from * 4 more times; end last repeat sl st in base of beginning ch.

Rnd 3: In first ch 4 space, *1 sc, 4 dc, 1 tr, 4 dc, 1 sc; repeat from * in each of the remaining ch 4 spaces; join with sl st to first sc.

Rnd 4: *Ch 5, sl st between next 2 sc (between petals); repeat from * 4 more times; end with sl st to base of beginning ch.

Note: Pull previous petal forward so ch lies behind.

Rnd 5: Ch 1 in each ch 5 space; *1 sc, 5 dc, 3 tr, 5 dc, 1 sc; repeat from * around, end with sl st to beginning ch.

End yarn, leaving a tail of at least 6" to pull through loop.

DOUBLE-RUFFLED FLOWER

To begin: Ch 4; join with a sl st to first ch to form ring.

Rnd 1: Ch 2 (counts as 1 sc), work 11 sc into ring, join with sl st to beginning ch (12 sc including the ch 2).

Rnd 2: Working in front loop only of each sc, work (1 sc, ch 4, 1 sc) into each sc.

Rnd 3: Working into the back loop only of each sc of Rnd 1 work (1 sc, ch 6, 1 sc) into each sc.

End yarn, leaving a tail of at least 6" to pull through last loop.

SINGLE-RUFFLED FLOWER

To begin: Ch 4; join with a sl st to first ch to form ring.

Rnd 1: Ch 2 (counts as 1 sc), work 11 sc into ring, join with sl st to beginning ch (12 sc including the ch 2).

Rnd 2: Working in front loop only of each sc, work (1 sc, ch 4, 1 sc) into each sc.

End yarn, leaving a tail of at least 6" to pull through last loop.

FLOWER CENTER

To begin: Ch 3, *yo, insert hook into third ch from hook and pull through 2 loops; repeat from * 4 more times; yo, pull through all 6 loops on hook.

End yarn, leaving a tail of at least 6".

LARGE LEAF

To begin: Ch 12; sc in second ch from hook and in each of next 2 ch, hdc in each of next 2 ch, dc in each of next 3 ch, hdc in next ch, sc in next ch, 3 sc in last ch.

Working down the other side of the original ch 12, work 1 sc in next ch, 1 hdc in next ch, dc in each of next 3 ch, hdc in each of next 2 ch, then sc in each of last 3 ch.

End yarn, leaving a tail of about 6".

SMALL LEAF

To begin: Ch 9; sc in second ch from hook and in next ch, hdc in each of next 2 ch, dc in each of next 2 ch, hdc in next ch, 3 sc in last ch.

Working down the other side of the original ch 9, work 1 hdc in next ch, dc in each of next 2 ch, hdc in each of next 2 ch, then sc in each of last 2 ch.

End yarn, leaving a tail of about 6" to pull through last loop.

Assembling and Finishing

TANK WITH YELLOW FLOWER

With Yellow, make one double-ruffled flower. With Fern, make one large leaf, one small leaf, and one flower center.

Attach the flower center to the flower by drawing the tails through the center ring of the flower. Thread both tails through a sharp large-eye needle and sew the flowers onto the tank as in photo.

Using matching thread, sew leaves in place.

TANK WITH PINK FLOWER

With Blush, make one double-ruffled and one single-ruffled flower. With Fern, make one large leaf, two small leaves, and two flower centers.

Attach the flower centers to the flowers by drawing the tails through the center rings of the flowers. Thread both tails through a sharp large-eye needle and sew the flowers onto the tank as in photo.

Using matching thread, sew leaves in place.

TANK WITH PURPLE FLOWER

With Viola, make one large flat flower. With Fern, make one large leaf, one small leaf, and one flower center.

Attach the flower center to the flower by drawing the tails through the center ring of the flower. Thread both tails through a sharp large-eye needle and sew onto the tank.

Sew leaves in place.

It certainly doesn't look like Granny's old afghan, but it's made using exactly the same technique. I've just refreshed the look by turning it into a bright, totally wearable scarf in delicious colors. Snuggly enough for the worst winter weather, these grannies are cute and fashionable, and

red-hot granny scarf

they keep you bundled up against the cold. This vintage look is easy to achieve, and it's the perfect take-along project, as you're always working on separate little squares that get stitched together only at the end. Use my color scheme or try your own favorite combination.

red-hot granny scarf

SIZES One size

FINISHED MEASUREMENTS 9¾" x 65"

YARN

Matchmaker Merino DK by Jaeger, 100% merino wool, 1.75 oz (50 g)/130 yd (120 m) balls

   cc A Petal #883: 1 ball

   cc B Rosy #870: 1 ball

Kid Classic by Rowan, 70% lamb's wool/26% kid mohair/4% nylon, 1.75 oz (50 g)/151 yd (140 m) balls

   cc C Pinched #819: 1 ball

   cc D Juicy #827: 1 ball

MATERIALS

Hook: Size G/6 (4 mm), *or size needed to obtain gauge.*

Large-eye yarn needle

GAUGE

Basic granny square = 3¼" square
Take time to make sure your gauge is correct.

ABBREVIATIONS AND TECHNIQUES

Chain	**ch**	(p. 22)
Contrasting color	**cc**	
Double crochet	**dc**	(p. 26)
Granny squares		(p. 89)
Single crochet	**sc**	(p. 24)
Slip stitch	**sl st**	(p. 69)

PATTERN STITCH

To begin: Ch 4; join ch with a sl st to form a ring.

Rnd 1 (right side): Ch 3 (counts as 1 dc), work 2 dc into ring, ch 1. *Work 3 dc into ring, ch 1; repeat from * twice more.

Join round with a sl st in third ch of ch 3. End yarn.

Join next color with a sl st in any ch 1 space.

Rnd 2: Ch 3, work 2 dc in same ch 1 space, ch 1, *work (3 dc, ch 1, 3 dc for corner space) in next ch 1 space, ch 1; repeat from * twice more. End with 3 dc in beginning ch space, ch 1.

Join round with a sl st in third ch of ch 3. End yarn.

Join next color with a sl st in any ch 1 space that isn't a corner.

Rnd 3: Ch 3, work 2 dc in same ch 1 space, ch 1, *work (3 dc, ch 1, 3 dc) in next ch 1 space, ch 1, work 3 dc in next ch 1 space, ch 1; repeat from * twice more. End with (3 dc, ch 1, 3 dc) in last corner, ch 1.

Join round with a sl st in third ch of ch 3. End yarn.

THE SCARF

Following the Pattern Stitch (page 98), crochet 60 granny squares, 10 each worked in the color sequences shown in the chart below.

	A	B	C	D	E	F
Round 1	cc D	cc A	cc C	cc D	cc B	cc C
Round 2	cc C	cc C	cc A	cc A	cc A	cc D
Round 3	cc A	cc D	cc B	cc B	cc C	cc A

FINISHING

Weave in all loose ends.

To assemble the squares, begin by creating rows of three squares each: For Row 1, sew one A square to one B square to one C square. (Follow the instructions for sewing vertical seams on page 33 for stitching technique.)

Next, sew one D square to one E square to one F square.

Repeat these two rows until you have 20 rows of three squares each.

Stitch the rows together, alternating the A, B, C rows with the D, E, F rows.

Join cc C with a sl st to any corner and work sc in the first st; *dc in the next st, sc in each of the next 2 sts; repeat from * around entire scarf. Join round with a sl st in first sc.

End yarn, draw tail through loop. Weave all loose ends into back of scarf.

Beyond Pink and Red

If you'd like to try another color combination, assign a color letter to each of your new yarn choices. For example, cc A = blue, cc B = turquoise, cc C = violet, cc D = purple. Then you can follow the color sequences given in my chart to achieve a balanced pattern that still has variety.

Perfectly whimsical, with a flirty flapper appeal, this sweet mohair cloche is a hat you'll want to make again and again. Fuzzy yarn and a large hook make this project so easy and fast you'll need one to match every coat you own. A single bloom (crocheted separately) hangs low over the ear for a sassy look with just the right amount of panache. You'll be looking forward to the coldest days for an excuse to top off your outfit with this chic head warmer. This project gives you a chance to try out your shaping skills, as well as to work in a circle.

mohair flapper hat

mohair flapper hat

SIZE One size

FINISHED MEASUREMENTS 21" circumference

YARN Mohair Classic by Berroco, 78% mohair/13% wool/
9% nylon, 1½ oz (43 g)/93 yd (85 m) balls

- #A6408: 2 balls

MATERIALS

Hook: Size I/9 (5.5 mm), *or size needed to obtain gauge*

Large-eye yarn needle

GAUGE

8 sts = 4" (10 cm) in dc

6 rows = 4" (10 cm) in dc

Take time to make sure your gauge is correct.

ABBREVIATIONS AND TECHNIQUES

Chain	**ch**	(p. 22)
Crocheted flower		(p. 90)
Decrease	**dec**	(p. 68)
Double crochet	**dc**	(p. 26)
Single crochet	**sc**	(p. 24)
Slip stitch	**sl st**	(p. 69)
Stitch(es)	**st(s)**	

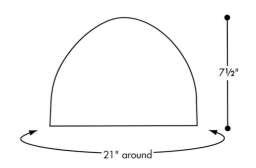

7½"

21" around

Finished Hat Measurements

Crocheting the Hat

To begin: Ch 43; sc in second ch from hook and each ch across (42 sc). Taking care not to twist ch, join to form a circle, ch 3, turn.

Working in the round, *but turning at the end of each round so that you work back and forth,* dc in each st around; sl st in top of turning ch to join (42 dc). Ch 3, turn.

Work 3 more rounds in dc, then shape the hat as follows.

Rnd 1: *Dc in next 4 sts, then work next 2 dc tog (dec); repeat from * around (35 dc), join, ch 3, turn.

Rnd 2: *Dc in the next 5 sts, then work next 2 dc tog (dec); repeat from * around (30 dc), join, ch 3, turn.

Rnd 3: Repeat Rnd 1 (25 dc), join, ch 3, turn.

Rnd 4: *Dc in next 3 sts, then work next 2 dc tog (dec); repeat from * around (20 dc), join, ch 3, turn.

Rnd 5: *Dc in next 2 sts, then work next 2 dc tog (dec); repeat from * around (15 dc), join, ch 3, turn.

Rnd 6: *Dc in next 2 sts, then work next 2 dc tog (dec); repeat from * around, ending dc in next st, then work last 2 dc tog (dec) (11 dc), join, ch 3, turn.

Row 7: *Work next 2 dc tog (dec); repeat from * around, ending dc in last dc (6 dc).

End yarn leaving a long tail. Thread tail through a large-eye needle, insert the needle into the top of each of the remaining dc, and draw the tail through to pull the circle together. Weave in ends.

Crocheting the Flower

To begin: Ch 5; join with sl st to first ch to form ring.

Rnd 1: Ch 2 (counts as 1 sc), work 15 sc into ring, join with sl st to beg ch (16 sc).

Rnd 2: *Ch 4, skip 2 sc, sl st in next sc; repeat from * 4 more times; end last repeat sl st in base of beginning ch.

Rnd 3: In each ch 4 space around work, (1 sc, 4 dc, 1 tr, 4 dc, 1 sc); join with sl st to first sc.

Rnd 4: [Ch 5, sl st between next 2 sc (between petals)] 5 times, end sl st to base of beg ch.

Rnd 5: Ch 1, in each ch 5 space, work (1 sc, 5 dc, 3 tr, 5 dc, 1 sc) around; end sl st to beginning ch.

End yarn.

FINISHING

Weave in all loose ends.

Use project yarn and a large-eye yarn needle to sew flower onto side of hat as shown in photo.

Flapper hat flower

completely
HOOK

Sophisticated and sexy, this dress is as much fun to make as it is wear. It's as elegant as you need it to be worn with strappy heels and a little satin clutch, or try slipping it over jeans or Capri pants for a funky '70s look. Crocheted in a dreamy, silvery pink ribbon yarn, the fitted bodice and

posh frock

plenty of stretch make this a truly versatile, not to mention comfortable, little frock. Perfect for any festive occasion you can dream up. Stitch up a simple tube lining in a matching color, or wear it over a pretty vintage slip of the same length. Once you've gotten used to the feel of it, ribbon is fun — and fast — to crochet with!

posh frock

SIZES	SMALL	MEDIUM	LARGE
FINISHED MEASUREMENTS			
• Bust	34"	37"	40"
• Length	32"	35"	38"

YARN Tartelette by Knit One Crochet Too, 50% cotton/40% Tactel nylon/10% nylon, 1.75 oz (50g)/75 yd (68m) skeins

	SMALL	MEDIUM	LARGE
• Pink Grapefruit #211	7 skeins	8 skeins	10 skeins

MATERIALS

Hook: Size K/10½ (6.5 mm), *or size needed to obtain gauge*
Large-eye yarn needle
1 (1¼, 1¼) yds 54" wide slip fabric
Matching thread
Sewing needle
1¼ yds ½" wide elastic

GAUGE

10 sts = 4" in dc
6 rows = 4" in dc
Take time to make sure your gauge is correct.

ABBREVIATIONS AND TECHNIQUES

Chain	**ch**	(p. 22)
Double crochet	**dc**	(p. 26)
Increase	**inc**	(p. 69)
Single crochet	**sc**	(p. 24)
Slip stitch	**sl st**	(p. 69)
Triple crochet	**tr**	(p. 30)

BODICE

To begin: Ch **85** (**95**, **103**); dc in fourth ch from hook and in each ch across [**82** (**92**, **100**) dc]; join to form a circle.

Note: Be careful not to twist the chain when you form the circle.

Rnd 1: Ch 3, turn. Dc in each st around, sl st in turning ch to join. Ch 3, turn.

Repeat last round until piece measures **6** (**6½**, **7**) inches. End yarn.

FRONT

Join yarn with sl st on the **8th** (**9th**, **10th**) st from where you ended the yarn, ch 3, then working in dc, work across next **26** (**29**, **31**) sts, ch 3, turn.

Work 1 more row in dc, ch 3, turn.

STRAPS

Keeping in dc, work across **4** (**4**, **5**) sts, and then continue working on these sts until strap measures 12". End yarn.

Skip center **19** (**22**, **22**) sts, join yarn with sl st on next st, ch 3, and work in dc across next **3** (**3**, **4**) sts. Work in dc across **4** (**4**, **5**) sts [the ch 3 and 3 (3, 4) stitches worked in previous row] until strap measures 12". End yarn.

Note: Count rows to make certain straps are the same length.

BACK

With right side facing, join yarn with sl st on **15th** (**17th**, **19th**) st from left front (armhole), ch 3, then work in dc across next **26** (**29**, **31**) sts, ch 3, turn.

SKIRT

Turn work and join yarn at bottom of bodice where you began.

Work 1 round sc, inc 1 st every **5th** (**6th**, **6th**) st **16** (**15**, **16**) times, noting that the last **2** (**2**, **4**) sts are worked in sc [**98** (**107**, **116**) sts].

Rnd 1: Working in the round but turning at the end of each round so that you work back and forth, ch 5 (counts as tr, ch 1), *skip 1 st, tr, ch 1. Repeat from * around, ending with sl st into fourth ch of ch 5, ch 5, turn.

Rnd 2: Work Rnd 1 once more, ch 5, turn.

Rnd 3: Skip 1 st *tr, ch 1, skip 1 ch, tr, ch 2, skip 1 ch; repeat from * around, ending by joining with sl st into fourth ch of ch 5, ch 5, turn.

Repeat Rnd 3 until piece measures **32** (**35**, **38**) inches from shoulder or desired length; ch 1, turn. Sc in each tr and ch around; join.

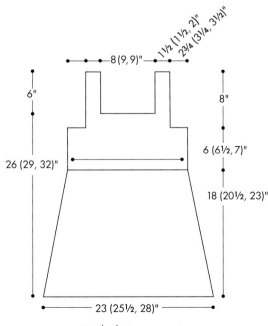

Finished Measurements

Rnd 4: Skip 1 st, *tr, ch 1, skip 1 ch, tr, ch 2, skip 2 ch; repeat from * around.

End by joining with st into fourth ch of ch 5. Ch 5, turn. End yarn.

FINISHING

With right side facing, attach yarn at underarm; sc evenly around edge of armhole; join. Repeat for other armhole. Attach yarn at back edge of strap; sc evenly around neck. Sl st to join.

Making a Tube Slip

1. Cut slip fabric to width and length of skirt, adding 4" to length and 1" to width. With right sides facing, fold in half lengthwise. Sew back seam with a ½" seam allowance.

2. To make casing for elastic, turn down ¼" around top; press in place. Turn down again 1" and stitch close to first fold, leaving a 1" opening to insert the elastic. Insert elastic through casing and sew ends together securely.

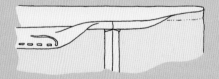

3. Hem bottom edge of lining to desired length, about 1" shorter than the skirt.

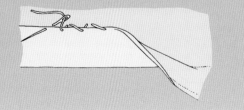

Completely classic yet infinitely cool, the Chanel-inspired jacket never goes out of style. With crisp, graphic lines and a time-honored color combination of bold black and white, this tailored jacket is perfect over either low-slung jeans or a hipster skirt. Bulky yarn and a large hook make

designer jacket

this project go much faster than you might guess. The white detailing is woven in after the crocheting is done. Although this is a big project, it's a relatively easy one. If you've gotten comfortable with shaping and following a pattern, you'll be delighted at how quickly it goes — and how incredible the results are.

designer jacket

SIZES	SMALL	MEDIUM	LARGE
FINISHED MEASUREMENTS			
•Chest	35"	38"	40"
•Length	19"	20"	21"

YARN Zoom by Classic Elite
Yarns, 50% alpaca/50% wool,
1.75 oz (50 g)/52 yd (45 m) skeins

•Black #013	14 skeins	16 skeins	18 skeins
•White #016	2 skeins	2 skeins	2 skeins

MATERIALS

Hook: Size I/9 (5.5 mm), *or size needed to obtain gauge*
Large-eye yarn needle

GAUGE

10 sts = 4" in sc; 12 rows = 4" in sc
Make sure your gauge is correct.

ABBREVIATIONS AND TECHNIQUES

Chain	**ch**	(p. 22)
Decrease	**dec**	(p. 68)
Increase	**inc**	(p. 69)
Single crochet	**sc**	(p. 24)
Stitch(es)	**st(s)**	

BACK

To begin: Ch **45** (**49**, **51**); sc in second ch from hook and in each ch across [**44** (**48**, **50**) sc].

Work even until piece measures **11** (**11½**, **12**) inches. End yarn.

BACK ARMHOLE

Skip 5 sts, then join yarn again on sixth st, sc across **34** (**38**, **40**) sts. Remaining 5 sts are unworked.

Work even until piece measures 18½ (19½, **20½**) inches.

Work across **8** (**9**, **10**) sts. End yarn.

Skip middle **18** (**20**, **20**) sts, join yarn, and work across remaining **8** (**9**, **10**) sts. End yarn.

RIGHT FRONT

To begin: Ch **23** (**25**, **26**); sc in second ch from hook and in each ch across [**22** (**24**, **25**) sc].

Work even until piece measures **11** (**11½**, **12**) inches. End yarn.

FRONT ARMHOLE

Skip 5 sts, then join yarn again on the sixth st, sc across **17** (**19**, **20**) sts.

Work even until piece measures **15** (**16**, **16½**) inches, ending ready for a right-side row.

NECK

Row 1: Work across **13** (**15**, **16**) sts, turn. Leave remaining 4 sts unworked.

Row 2: Work next 2 sts tog (dec), work remaining **12** (**14**, **15**) sts.

Continue to dec 1 st at neck edge as in Row 2 every row **4** (**5**, **5**) more times. You will have [**8** (**9**, **10**) sts].

Work even until front is same length as back. End yarn.

LEFT FRONT

Work as for Right Front, reversing the shaping.

SLEEVES (MAKE 2)

To begin: Ch **22** (**24**, **24**); sc in second ch from hook and in each ch across [**21** (**23**, **23**) sc].

Working in sc, inc 1 st each side every 4 rows **10** (**10**, **12**) times. You will have [**41** (**43**, **47**) sts]. (For instruction on how to increase, see page 69.)

Work even until piece measures **18** (**19**, **20**) inches. End yarn.

ASSEMBLING THE JACKET

Before sewing the pieces together, weave in the decorative stitching, following instructions below.

Place fronts and back on a flat surface, right side facing down. Following instructions on page 33 for sewing horizontal seams, stitch shoulder seams.

With right sides facing down, match sleeve centers to shoulder seams. Pin sleeves to jacket; distance from armholes to bottom edge must be same on front and back. Stitch, using technique for horizontal seams. Sew side and sleeve underarm seams. Turn garment right-side out.

Beginning at right side seam, weave decorative stitching along all edges of jacket, 1 stitch (or 1 row) in from edge. End yarn. Repeat at bottom edges of sleeves.

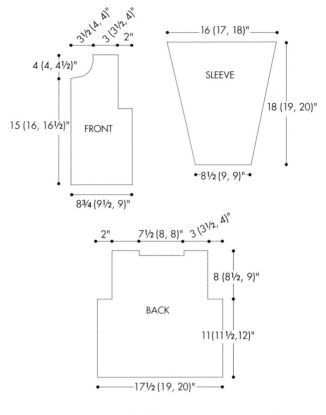

Final Measurements

Decorative Stitching

Before sewing jacket pieces together, weave in decorative stitching as follows: Thread a large-eye yarn needle with white yarn. Beginning on right front, 5 rows up from bottom edge, weave over 1 stitch and under next across jacket, from side to front edge. Stay within same crochet row. Carry yarn along front edge of jacket on wrong side, catching stitches without allowing white to show on right side. Go up 5 rows, then weave back to side edge, as for first line of weaving. Continue to weave in this manner every 5 rows to shoulder. Repeat on left front. Before weaving on back and sleeves, lay out jacket as it will be assembled and mark where weaving should

begin so that rows align properly. Complete weaving on back and sleeves.

For vertical stitching, start at bottom right front, 3 stitches in from front edge. Weave over 1 row and under next from bottom to neck edge. Carry yarn along edge for 5 stitches, then weave to bottom edge in same manner. Complete vertical weaving on all pieces.

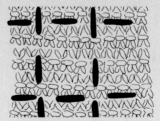

A terrific, easy-to-wear skirt. Whether on a romantic walk in the park or at a stylish garden party, you'll love showing off this versatile garment. The tiny pearl buttons and little tie at the waist add to its charm. In cooler weather, tights, knee-high boots, and a lacy vintage slip give the skirt a totally different look, making it a great any-season addition to your wardrobe. It's definitely a more advanced project, but don't let the pattern intimidate you. Once you have the hang of the few pattern stitches, you simply use them over and over to complete the skirt. It's quite simple to adjust the length, so you can make it as short or as long as you like.

chic hippie skirt

chic hippie skirt

SIZES	SMALL	MEDIUM	LARGE
FINISHED MEASUREMENTS			
• Waist	28"	30"	32"
• Hip	34"	37"	40"

YARN Cotton Classic by
Tahki/Stacy Charles,
100% cotton, 1.75 oz
(50 g)/108 yd (100 m) balls

• #3712	10 skeins	12 skeins	14 skeins

MATERIALS

Hook: For yoke and shell stitch skirt,
size G/6 (4 mm), *or size needed to
obtain gauge;* for yoke edging, size F/5
(3.75 mm)
Large-eye yarn needle
4 small buttons

GAUGE

16 sts = 4" in dc
8 rows = 4" in dc
*Take time to make sure your gauge is
correct.*

ABBREVIATIONS AND TECHNIQUES

Chain	**ch**	(p. 22)
Double crochet	**dc**	(p. 26)
Single crochet	**sc**	(p. 24)
Slip stitch	**sl st**	(p. 69)

PATTERN STITCHES

3-DC Shell: Work 3 dc in center dc of
previous shell.
5-DC Shell: Work 5 dc in center dc of
previous shell.

YOKE

To begin: Ch **115** (**123**, **131**); dc in fourth ch
from hook and in each ch across [**112** (**120**, **128**)
dc], ch 3, turn.

Rows 1–4: Dc in each dc across, ch 3, turn.

Rows 5, 7, 9: Dc in each dc across, increasing
4 (**6**, **8**) sts evenly spaced in each row; ch 3, turn.

Rows 6, 8, 10: Dc in each dc, ch 3, turn.

Row 11: Dc in each dc across, increasing **4** (**6**, **8**)
sts evenly spaced across row [you will have **128**
(**144**, **160**) sts]. Sl st in top of ch 3 turning st
from Row 10 to form a circle. Ch 3, turn.

SHELL STITCH SKIRT

Note: For 3-DC and 5-DC Shells, see at left.

Row 12: *Dc in dc, skip 1 dc, 3-DC Shell in next
dc, skip 1 dc; repeat from * around. Sl st in top
of ch 3 to join. [You will have **32** (**36**, **40**) 3-DC
Shells]. Ch 3, turn.

Row 13: *Dc in each dc, 3-DC Shell in center dc
of each shell; repeat from * around; join, ch 3, turn.

Row 14: *Dc in each dc, ch 1, 3-DC Shell in center dc of each shell, ch 1; repeat from * around;
join, ch 3, turn.

Rows 15–21: Work even in established pattern (dc in each dc, ch 1, 3-DC Shell, ch 1). Join at end of each row, ch 3, turn.

Row 22: *Dc in dc, ch 1, 5-DC Shell in center dc of next shell, ch 1, (dc in dc, ch 1, 3-DC Shell in center dc of shell, ch 1) 7 times; repeat from * around.
Medium size only: Work as for small size to last 4 shells. *Dc in dc, ch 1, 3-DC Shell in center dc of shell, ch 1; repeat from * to end. [You will have **4** 5-DC Shells and **32** 3-DC Shells.]

Rows 23–29: Work in established pattern (dc in each dc, ch 1, 5-DC or 3-DC Shell in appropriate shells, ch 1), joining at end of each row; ch 3, turn.

Row 30: *Dc in dc, ch 1, 5-DC Shell in center dc of 5-DC Shell, ch 1, (dc in dc, ch 1, 3-DC Shell in center dc of shell, ch 1) 3 times. Repeat from * around. [You will have **8** (**9**, **10**) 5-DC Shells and **24** (**27**, **30**) 3-DC Shells.]

Rows 31–37: Work in established pattern (dc in each dc, ch 1, 5-DC or 3-DC Shell in appropriate shells, ch 1), joining at end of each row; ch 3, turn.

Row 38: *Dc in dc, ch 1, 5-DC Shell in center dc of 5-DC Shell, ch 1, dc in dc, ch 1, 3-DC Shell in center dc of shell, ch 1. Repeat from * around. [You will have **16** (**18**, **20**) 5-DC Shells and **16** (**18**, **20**) 3-DC Shells.]

Rows 39–50 (or desired length): Work even in established pattern (dc in each dc, ch 1, 5-DC or 3-DC Shell in appropriate shells, ch 1), joining at end of each row and ending with a right-side row; ch 3, turn.

Last row: With wrong side facing, sc in each st or ch around.

DRAWSTRING

Ch **151** (**161**, **171**); sc in second ch and each ch across to end. End yarn and weave in ends.

Beginning at back edge of top row, weave over and under every 2 dc to other edge.

YOKE EDGING

Row 1: With right side facing and smaller hook, attach yarn at right bottom of yoke opening. Sc evenly up edge of yoke to corner, 3 sc in corner, **112** (**122**, **130**) sc to next corner, 3 sc in corner, sc back to bottom of yoke. The number of sts on left and right sides should be equal. Ch 1, turn.

Row 2: Sc in each sc around, working 3 sc in center sc of corner sts. Ch 1, turn.

Note: Mark right yoke for 4 buttonholes, with top button at yoke top and remaining 3 buttons evenly spaced to bottom.

Row 3: *Sc to marker, ch 1, skip 1; repeat from * to top of yoke, sc all remaining sts. Do not turn.

Row 4: Working from left to right, sc in each st and space around. End yarn.

FINISHING

Sew buttons opposite buttonholes. Lap right side of yoke over left and tack lower edges together.

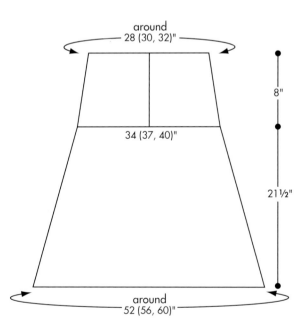

Finished Measurements

be jeweled

Vintage-inspired but thoroughly modern, these crocheted chokers are the easiest things you've ever fashioned with a crochet hook. Sweet and sassy, they're a cinch to make and open to endless experimentation — adorn them with unique treasures, such as old beads, baubles, or buttons. These necklaces are perfect for using up scraps, as well as trying out an expensive novelty yarn that you might not want to use on a larger project. It's fun to experiment with different yarns for totally different effects. The pattern for the flower pin is on page 91. Use it as a whimsical detail on your favorite cardigan, a dramatic cluster on the lapel of a coat, or a dainty bloom on a chic knit hat.

be jeweled

COTTON NECKLACE WITH BEADS

SIZES One size

YARN Grace by Patons, 100% mercerized cotton, 1.75 oz (50 g)/136 yd (125 m) balls
  • Ruby #60409: 1 ball

MATERIALS

Hook: Size F/5 (3.75 mm), *or size needed to obtain gauge*
20 amber beads
Small-eye yarn needle

GAUGE

20 sts = 4" in sc
26 rows = 4" in sc
Take time to make sure your gauge is correct.

ABBREVIATIONS AND TECHNIQUES

Chain	**ch**	(p. 22)
Double crochet	**dc**	(p. 26)
Single crochet	**sc**	(p. 24)

To begin: With yarn needle, strand 20 beads on yarn.

Ch 50. Pull up a bead, * ch 3, pull up bead; repeat from * 9 more times. Ch 51, turn.

Sc in second ch from hook and in next 48 ch.

*Work dc in the next 2 ch, slip bead, ch 1, dc in the next 2 ch (between beads of previous row); repeat from * 9 more times; sc to end.

FINISHING

Weave in ends.

FUR NECKLACE

SIZES One size

YARN Fun Fur by Lion Brand Yarn, 60% cotton/40% microfiber, 1.75 oz (50 g)/98 yd (90 m) skeins
  • Violet #191: 1 skein

MATERIALS

Hook: Size I/9 (5.5 mm), *or size needed to obtain gauge*

GAUGE

12 sts = 4" in sc
14 rows = 4" in sc
Take time to make sure your gauge is correct.

ABBREVIATIONS AND TECHNIQUES

Chain	**ch**	(p. 22)
Double crochet	**dc**	(p. 26)
Single crochet	**sc**	(p. 24)

To begin: Ch 52; sc in second ch from hook and in the next 16 ch.

*Dc, ch2, skip 2; repeat from * 5 more times; dc in next ch; sc in each ch to end.

FINISHING

Weave in ends.

SUEDE NECKLACE

SIZES One size

YARN: Suede by Berroco, 100% nylon,
1.75 oz (50 g)/120 yd (110 m) balls
- Hopalong Cassidy #3714: 1 ball

MATERIALS

Hook: Size H/8 (5 mm), *or size needed to obtain gauge*
3 turquoise beads
Small-eye yarn needle

GAUGE

18 sts = 4" in sc
22 rows = 4" in sc
Take time to make sure your gauge is correct.

ABBREVIATIONS AND TECHNIQUES

Chain	**ch**	(p. 22)
Double crochet	**dc**	(p. 26)
Single crochet	**sc**	(p. 24)

To begin: With yarn needle, strand 3 beads on yarn.

Ch 50; pull up a bead, *ch 3, pull up bead; repeat from * 2 more times, ch 51, turn.

Sc in second ch from hook and in the next 40 ch.

*Dc, ch 1, skip 1; repeat from * 3 more times; dc.

*Ch 1, skip bead, work dc in each of the next 2 ch; repeat from * 2 more times.

*Dc, ch 1, skip 1; repeat from * 3 more times; dc, sc to end.

FINISHING
Weave in ends.

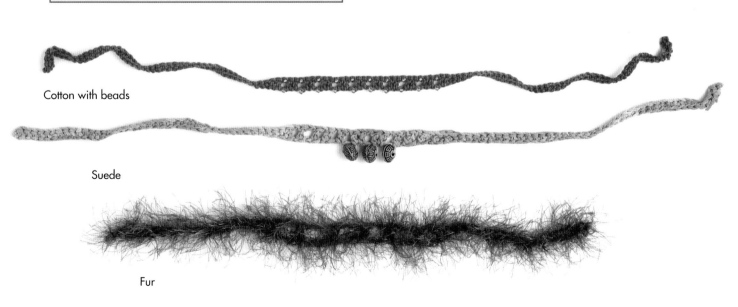

Cotton with beads

Suede

Fur

hooking your
NEST

I told you that there would be no end to the delightful uses for crocheted blossoms! Inspired by the summery scent of freshly washed linens drying in the sun, these charming flower motifs and lacy edgings will brighten your bathroom and transform plain, boring towels into hard-to-

vintage embellishments

find vintage pieces. Once you master this project, you'll be adding posies and edgings to your sheets and pillowcases, too. The edgings and flowers are made with a light-weight cotton yarn in lovely spring colors. Of course, you may use colors to coordinate with your own towels and bath.

vintage embellishments

SIZES

- 16" wide hand towel
- 24" wide hand towel

YARN 4-Ply Cotton by Rowan, 100% cotton, 1.75 oz (50 g)/185 yd (170 m) balls

- ■ Fresh #131: 1 ball
- ■ Flirty #127: 1 ball
- ■ Bluebell #136: 1 ball

MATERIALS

Hook: Size F/5 (3.75 mm), *or size needed to obtain gauge*
Sharp large-eye yarn needle
One 24" towel
Two 16" hand towels

GAUGE

16 sts = 4" in sc
20 rows = 4" in sc
Note: Even though you aren't creating a flat piece of fabric, you may want to work a 6" square gauge swatch to ensure the right-size flowers and edging.

ABBREVIATIONS AND TECHNIQUES

Chain	**ch**	(p. 22)
Crocheted flowers		(p. 90)
Double crochet	**dc**	(p. 26)
Half double crochet	**hdc**	(p. 28)
Single crochet	**sc**	(p. 24)
Slip stitch	**sl st**	(p. 69)
Yarn over	**yo**	(p. 68)

EDGING PATTERN STITCH

Row 1: *Skip 2 sc, 5 dc in next st, skip 2 sc, hdc in next st; repeat from * across, ch 2, turn.

Row 2: *Hdc in hdc from previous row, work 5 dc in center dc of previous row; repeat from * across, ch 2, turn.

Row 3: Repeat Row 2.

Crocheting the Flowers and Leaves

FLOWER #1

To begin: Ch 4, join with sl st to first ch to form ring.

Rnd 1: Ch 2 (counts as 1 sc), work 11 sc into the ring, then join with sl st to beginning ch (12 sc including the ch 2).

Rnd 2: *Working in front loop only* of each sc, work (1 sc, ch 4, 1 sc) into each sc.

Rnd 3: *Working into the back loop only* of each sc of Rnd 1, work *(1 sc, ch 6, 1 sc) in next sc, work (1 sc, ch 4, 1 sc) in next sc; repeat from * to end. End yarn and leave a tail of at least 6".

FLOWER #2

To begin: Ch 4, join with sl st to first ch to form ring.

Rnd 1: Ch 2 (counts as 1 sc), work 11 sc into the ring, then join with sl st to beginning ch (12 sc including the ch 2).

Rnd 2: *Working in front loop only* of each sc, work (1 sc, ch 4, 1 sc) into each sc. End yarn and leave a tail of at least 6".

FLOWER CENTER

To begin: Ch 3; *yo, insert hook into third ch from hook, and pull through 2 loops; repeat from * 4 more times, yo, pull through all 6 loops on hook.

Cut yarn, leaving a tail of at least 6", and pull through last loop.

LARGE LEAF

To begin: Ch 12; sc in second ch from hook and in each of next 2 ch, hdc in each of next 2 ch, dc in each of next 3 ch, hdc in next ch, sc in next ch, 3 sc in last ch.

Working down the other side of the original chain, work 1 sc in 1st ch, 1 hdc in next ch, dc in each of next 3 ch, hdc in each of next 2 ch, then sc in each of last 3 ch. End yarn and leave a tail of about 6".

SMALL LEAF

To begin: Ch 9; sc in second ch from hook and in next ch, hdc in each of next 2 ch, dc in each of next 2 ch, hdc in next ch, 3 sc in the last ch.

Working down the other side of the original ch, work 1 hdc in 1st ch, dc in each of next 2 ch, hdc in each of next 2 ch, then sc in each of last 2 ch. End yarn and leave a tail of about 6".

Making and Assembling

PINK TOWEL (24")

Flower #1: Make two with Flirty.

Flower #2: Make one with Flirty; make two with Bluebell.

Leaves: Make two large and two small with Fresh.

Flower center: Make five with Fresh.

Edging: With Flirty, ch 97; sc in second ch from hook and in each ch across (96 ch). Begin Edging Pattern Stitch and continue until you have completed all 3 rows. End yarn.

GREEN TOWEL (16")

Flower #1: Make one with Flirty.

Flower #2: Make two with Bluebell.

Leaves: Make two large and one small with Fresh.

Flower center: Make three with Fresh.

Edging: With Fresh, ch 61; sc in second ch from hook and in each ch across (60 sc). Begin Edging Pattern Stitch and continue until you have completed all 3 rows. End yarn.

BLUE TOWEL (16")

Flower #1: Make one with Flirty and one with Bluebell.

Flower #2: Make one with Flirty.

Leaves: Make one large and two small with Fresh.

Flower center: Make three with Fresh.

Edging: With Bluebell, ch 61; sc in second ch from hook and in each ch across (60 sc). Begin the Edging Pattern Stitch and continue until you have completed 2 rows. End yarn.

Final Touches

Using the yarn color that matches edging, attach edging to bottom of towel using blanket stitch. (See illustration.)

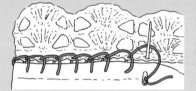

Sew flower center to each flower by drawing the tail through flower ring. Sew flowers and leaves in place as shown in photo.

With Fresh, embroider vines and stems to connect the flowers and leaves, using the photo for reference.

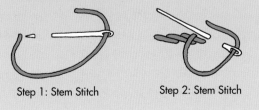

Step 1: Stem Stitch   Step 2: Stem Stitch

Whether you're looking for a sleek, modern statement or a more traditional accent for your home, the rich tones and geometric shapes of this large throw pillow make it a smart, stylish addition to any living room. The bold diamond design makes an impact without distracting, and the yarn — an

diamond square pillow

opulent blend of wool, kid mohair, and alpaca — adds just the right deluxe touch. The individual diamonds are created using bobbins, so you don't have to carry yarns across the width, making this a much easier piece to crochet than it looks.

diamond square pillow

SIZES One size

FINISHED MEASUREMENTS 16" × 16"

YARN Julia by Goddess Yarns, 50% wool/25% kid mohair/25% alpaca, 1.75 oz (50 g)/93 yd (87 m) balls

Natural #0010: 1 ball

Gold #2163: 1 ball

French Pumpkin #2250:1 ball

Rock Henna #2230: 3 balls

Purple Basil #3158: 1 ball

Lady's Mantle #3961: 1 ball

Velvet Moss #6086: 1 ball

Blue Thyme #4936: 1 ball

Deep Blue Sea #6396: 1 ball

MATERIALS

Hook: Size H/8 (5 mm), *or size needed to obtain gauge*

Large-eye yarn needle

16" × 16" pillow form

9 large yarn bobbins

GAUGE

13 sts = 4" in sc

18 rows = 4" in sc

Take time to make sure your gauge is correct.

ABBREVIATIONS AND TECHNIQUES

Chain	**ch**	(p. 22)
Changing colors		(p. 52)
Single crochet	**sc**	(p. 24)
Slip stitch	**sl st**	(p. 67)

FRONT

With Natural, ch 53. Starting with sc in second ch from hook, refer to chart for color sequence in each ch across (52 sc).

Working in sc throughout, continue to follow chart for color changes. End yarn.

With Natural, work 1 row of sc around the entire pillow (working 3 sc in each corner); join with a sl st. Change to Lady's Mantle and work 1 more row of sc around the pillow.

BACK

With Rock Henna, ch 57, then sc in second ch from hook and in each ch across (56 sc), ch 1, turn.

Work in sc on these sts until piece measures 16". End yarn.

FINISHING

Weave in ends on the wrong side of work.

Place pieces together, right sides facing, and follow directions on page 33 for sewing horizontal seams around 3 sides; leave a 10" opening on the fourth side.

Insert pillow form and sew up opening.

KEY TO COLORS

NATURAL
#0010

GOLD
#2163

FRENCH
PUMPKIN #2250

ROCK HENNA
#2230

PURPLE BASIL
#3158

LADY'S MANTLE
#3961

VELVET MOSS
#6086

BLUE THYME
#4936

DEEP BLUE SEA
#6396

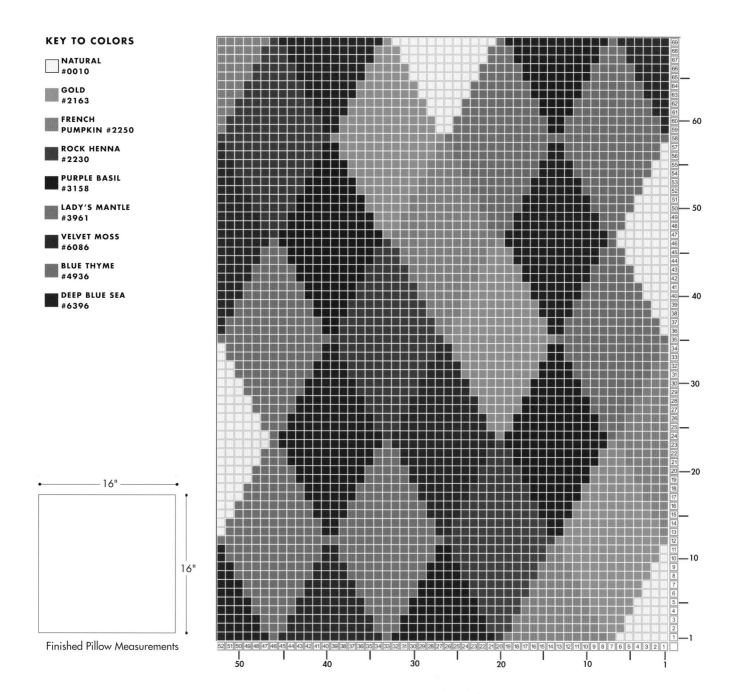

Finished Pillow Measurements

16"

16"

This easy lampshade embellishment will transform your dullest white shade into an unusual eye-catcher. That odd flea-market treasure that you haven't found just the right shade for will cast a romantic, old-fashioned glow dressed up in this netlike covering.

antique lampshade fringe

The look is completed by simple beaded fringe. I've used wooden beads, but the possibilities are endless, depending on the look you want to achieve. Try Victorian glass, Art Deco, or marbled beads for completely different effects.

antique lampshade fringe

SIZES One size

FINISHED MEASUREMENTS Approximately 10" wide at bottom

YARN Royale by Coats & Clark, 100% acrylic, 1.75 oz (50 g)/200 yd (185 m) balls
  • Yellow Green #2236: 1 ball

MATERIALS

Hook: Size H/8 (5 mm) *or size needed to obtain gauge*
Large-eye yarn needle
Lampshade with a diameter of 4" at top and 10" at bottom

GAUGE

16 sts = 4" in sc
20 rows = 4" in sc
Take time to make sure your gauge is correct.

ABBREVIATIONS AND TECHNIQUES

Chain	**ch**	(p. 22)
Double crochet	**dc**	(p. 26)
Single crochet	**sc**	(p. 24)
Slip stitch	**sl st**	(p. 69)

To begin: Ch 55; sc in second ch from hook and in each ch across (54 sc). Join to form a circle, taking care not to twist ch. Ch 7, turn.

Rnd 1: Skip 2 sc, *dc in next sc, ch 3, skip 2 sc; repeat from * around (18 dc including the first ch 7; join to fourth ch of ch 7.

Rnd 2: Ch 7, *dc in next dc, ch 3; repeat from * around; join to fourth ch of ch 7.

Rnd 3: Ch 7 *dc in next dc, ch 4; repeat from * around; join to fourth ch of ch 7.

Rnd 4: *Ch 12, skip (ch 4, dc, ch 4), sc in next dc; repeat from * around; sl st in base of ch 12. End yarn.

Rnd 5: Join yarn with sc in center of any ch 12 space. *Ch 14, sc into center of next ch 12 space; repeat from * around; sl st in base of ch 14. End yarn.

Rnd 6: Join yarn with sc in center of any ch 14 space. *Ch 12, sc into center of next ch 14 space; repeat from * around; sl st in base of ch 12. Ch 1, turn.

Rnd 7: Work 13 sc in each ch 12 space around; sl st to join to beginning sc. End yarn.

Rnd 8: Join yarn with sc to seventh sc of any 13 sc group of Rnd 7. *Ch 14, sc into seventh sc of next 13 sc group of previous rnd; repeat from * around; join. Ch 1, turn.

Rnd 9: Work 15 sc into each ch 14 space around; join. End yarn.

FINISHING

Weave in all loose ends.

Make nine 6-inch fringe and attach one in each ch 14 space around bottom. (See instructions on page 45 for making fringe.) Thread a bead onto each group of fringe and secure with an overhand knot.

String of Beads

Beads can be found at specialty bead shops, as well as at craft and sewing supply stores and online. If you save broken necklaces, incomplete sets of earrings, and other cast-off jewelry, you'll always have an interesting assortment of beads waiting for a new use. Because you may be working with relatively thick yarn rather than thread, look for beads with good-sized holes that the yarn will fit through.

Wherever you find beading supplies, you should also be able to obtain easy-to-thread, flexible needles that make the threading a simple procedure.

Perfectly suited to long, lazy days when there's nothing to do but spend the afternoon drifting in a hammock! And a hammock with this distinctive edging will get you dreaming that you're swinging between two palm trees in the Bahamas instead of in your own backyard. The

lazy-afternoon hammock

funky, macramé-style fringe is distinctive, and the heavyweight cotton yarn is sturdy enough to withstand the occasional downpour. Crocheted with a large hook, this project is quick and easy. Add ceramic or wooden beads for even more pizzazz.

lazy-afternoon hammock

SIZES One size

FINISHED MEASUREMENTS To fit hammock 60" long

YARN Aunt Lydia's Denim by Coats & Clark,
100% cotton, 400 yd (366 m) balls

• Milk #1002: 2 balls

MATERIALS

Hook: Size J/10 (6 mm), *or size needed to obtain gauge*
Large-eye yarn needle
Hammock

GAUGE

10 sts = 4" in dc
6 rows = 4" in dc
Take time to make sure your gauge is correct.

ABBREVIATIONS AND TECHNIQUES

Chain	**ch**	(p. 22)
Double crochet	**dc**	(p. 26)
Single crochet	**sc**	(p. 24)
Stitch(es)	**st(s)**	
Triple crochet	**tr**	(p. 30)

Crocheting the Edging

THE EDGING (MAKE 2)

To begin: Ch 152; dc in fourth ch from hook and in each st across (149 dc), ch 3, turn. Work one more row dc, ch 7, turn.

Row 1: Skip 4 dc, *tr in next st, ch 3, skip 3 sts; repeat from * across; tr in last st.

Row 2: *Ch 12, skip (ch 3, tr, ch 3), sc in next tr; repeat from * across. End with sc in fourth ch of ch 7 turning ch. Turn.

Row 3: *Ch 12, sc into center of previous ch 12 space; repeat from * across. End yarn. Turn.

Row 4: Join yarn in center of first ch 12, *ch 12, sc into center of next ch 12 space; repeat from * across, ch 2, turn.

Row 5: Work (sc, ch 1) 7 times into each ch 12 space across. End with sc in last st. End yarn.

Row 6: Join yarn in center sc of previous row, *ch 16, sc in center sc of next space; repeat from * across, ch 2, turn.

Row 7: (Sc, ch 1) 10 times into each ch 16 space; sc in last st. End yarn.

Note: Edging is figured for a 60" hammock. If your hammock is longer, ch 8 additional sts for each 3½" length.

Weave in all loose ends.

Make thirty-six 12" fringe (18 for each side) and attach to the bottom of the edging, referring to fringe directions on page 45.

Using the project yarn threaded in a large-eye yarn needle and an overcast stitch, sew edging to edge of hammock.

Repeat for second side of hammock.

The Perfect Hammock

In order to maximize lazy afternoons in your newly enhanced hammock, here are a few tips for some truly luxurious swinging.

- Make sure to hang your hammock in the right place. At the time of day you're most likely to be in it, check out the spot you're going to hang it. Are there problems with shade — too much or not enough? Is there a nearby flower that attracts a lot of bees? What's the view like? Too near noisy neighbors or busy traffic?
- Consider the height, taking into account any possible stretching that might occur. To give you enough clearance, most hammocks should be hung so the ends are about 4 feet from the ground.
- Security is crucial! You don't want to come tumbling down while napping. If you are hanging your hammock from a tree, avoid screwing a hook into the tree, which may damage the tree over time. Wrap double-braided nylon rope securely around the tree twice, then knot it using a fisherman's knot. Slip an S-hook into the knot and the other end of the S-hook into your hammock.
- Add pillows (crocheted or something a little more weather resistant) and a light shawl or throw for cooler afternoons and evenings.
- Hanging lights or setting up garden torches can turn your lazy afternoon into a romantic evening.
- Growing nearby plants with sweet, relaxing scents, such as hops and lavender, will make lounging in your hammock an extra-soothing treat.

Crochet Basics for Lefties

Learning a new skill from directions created for right-handers can be frustrating for lefties, so I'm hoping these adapted illustrations of the starting chain and single crochet will get you on your way. When you move on to more complex stitches, you may want to have a mirror image made of your illustrations at a copy store. Please respect copyright restrictions, and make copies for your own use only.

Making the Chain

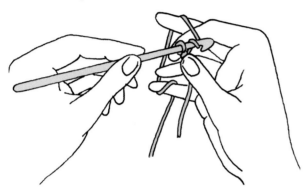

1. Bring the yarn over the hook from back to front, catch it with the hook, then pull it through the slip knot. It's important to slip the loop you've just made to the shank of the hook. If you leave it near the throat, the stitch will be too small.

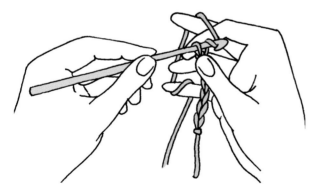

2. Repeat the process. Try to get a nice even tension. If you pull too hard, the chain will be too tight. If you don't give it enough tension, however, it will be too loose.

Single Crochet (sc)

Now that you're comfortable with the whole chain concept, let's start to learn some stitches. All crochet projects begin with a chain (ch), so you'll need to first chain (ch) 6 to practice the single crochet (sc). If you make a mistake, just pull out the stitches and start over. You aren't making anything yet — this is practice, and as I said, there are no crochet police watching you.

ROW 1

1. After making 6 chain stitches, begin the first row of single crochet by inserting the hook through the second chain from the hook.

2. Bring yarn over the hook from the back to the front.

3. Pull the yarn to the front and move it to the shank of the hook. There are now two loops on the hook.

4. Bring the yarn over the hook again from back to front and pull it through both loops on hook.

5. Now you have one loop on the hook, and you have completed 1 single crochet (sc).

6. Insert the hook into the next chain and repeat the process until you have reached the end of the chain. Do not crochet into the slip knot itself. You should see 5 stitches in the completed row. Don't forget to count as you work.

ROW 2

7. Before you turn to work a second row of single crochet, chain 1. This is called the *turning chain*. Now turn the piece counterclockwise so the back is facing you.

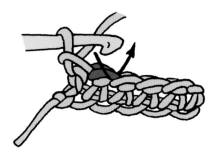

8. Work the first single crochet into the last single crochet of the previous row. This time, insert the hook under *both* top loops of the first single crochet, then repeat steps 2–5.

RESOURCES

Berroco, Inc.
14 Elmdale Road
P.O. Box 367
Uxbridge, MA 01569
1-508-278-2527
www.berroco.com

Classic Elite Yarns
122 Western Ave
Lowell, MA 01851
978-453-2837
www.classiceliteyarns.com

Coats & Clark
Consumer Services
P.O. Box 12229
Greenville, SC 29612-0229
1-800-648-1479
www.coatsandclark.com

Goddess Yarns
2911 Kavanaugh Blvd
Little Rock, AR 72205
1-866-332-9276
www.goddessyarns.com

Jaeger/Rowan
Westminster Fibers
4 Townsend West
Unit 8
Nashua, NH 03063
1-800-445-9276
www.knitrowan.com

Knit One Crochet Too
91 Tandberg Trail
Unit 6
Windham, ME 04062
1-800-357-7646
www.knitonecrochettoo.com

Patons
320 Livingstone Ave. South
Listowel, Ontario N4W 3H3
Canada
888-368-8401
www.patonsyarns.com

Tahki/Stacy Charles
70-30 80th Street
 Bld #36
Richwood, NY 11385
1-800-338-YARN
www.tahkistacycharles.com

INDEX

Page numbers in **bold** indicate a photograph; page numbers in *italic* indicate an illustration

Abbreviations, 18, 19, **19,** 34
Acrylic yarn, *16, 17*
Alpaca yarn, 14, *15*
Angora yarn, 14, *15*
Animal fibers, 14, *15*
Antique Lampshade Fringe, 132–35, *133–35*
Asterisk (*), 18–19

Baby Sweater, Candy Stripe, 78–81, *79–81*
Back loop, 18, *18*
Bags. *See* Purses
Bamboo Handle Purse, 54–57, *55–57*
Basic Scarf, 42–45, *43–45*
Beads, 135, *135*
Be Jeweled, 118–21, *119–21*
Bikini, Swimsuit Issue, 82–85, *83–85*
Black Wrap, Little, 70–73, *71–73*
Blocking, 33
Bracket symbols, 19
British hook sizes/terms, 11, **11,** 29
Bulky yarn, 17, *17*

Camel yarn, 14, *15*
Candy Stripe Baby Sweater, 78–81, *79–81*
Cashmere yarn, 14, *15*
Cell Phone Case, 38–41, *39–41*
Chain (ch), 22, *22,* 140, *140*
Chic Hippie Skirt, 114–17, *115–17*
Chokers, 118–21, *119–21*
Circles, 88–89, *88–89*
Color, 52–53, *52–53*
Continental (metric) hook sizes, 11, **11**
Cotton yarn, 12
Crochet, 9–35. *See also* Gauge; Stitches; Yarn

abbreviations, 18, 19, **19,** 34
circles, 88–89, *88–89*
color, 52–53, *52–53*
finishing, 32–33, *33,* 35, 113, *113*
flowers, 90–91, *90–91*
granny squares ("motifs"), 88–89, *88–89*
holding hook/yarn, 20–21, *20–21*
hook, *10,* 10–11, **11,** 20, *20*
joining yarn, 32, *32,* 52, *52*
language of, *18,* 18–19, 19, **29**
left-handers, 140–41, *140–41*
pattern, anatomy, 34–35, *34–35*
pattern stitches, 52–53, *53*
shaping/fitting, 68–69, *68–69*
sizing, 34
slip knot, 21, *21*
symbols, 18–19
Crochet bag, 18

Dagger symbol, 18–19
Decorative stitching, 113, *113*
Decrease (dec), 68–69, *68–69*
Designer Jacket, 110–13, *111–13*
Diamond Square Pillow, 128–31, *129–31*
Double crochet (dc), 26–27, *26–27,* 68, *68*
Dress, Posh Frock, 106–9, *107–9*

Egyptian cotton yarn, 12
Embellishments, Vintage, 124–27, *125–27*
English hook sizes/terms, 11, **11,** 29
Eyeglass Cases, 38–41, *39–41*
Eyelash yarn, 17

Finishing, 32–33, *33,* 35, 113, *113*
Fitting/shaping, 68–69, *68–69*
Flapper Mohair Hat, 100–103, *101–3*

Flowers, 90–91, *90–91*
Fringe, 45, *45,* 57, *57*
Fringe, Antique Lampshade, 132–35, *133–35*
Frock, Posh, 106–9, *107–9*
Front loop, 18, *18*

Gauge, 19
checking, 23, *23*
color of yarn impact on, 61
hook size and, 11, **11**
pattern, anatomy, 34
yarn label, 41, *41*
Granny Scarf, Red-Hot, 96–99, *97–98,* **99**
Granny squares ("motifs"), 88–89, *88–89*
Grip of hook, 10, *10*

Half double crochet (hdc), 28–29, *28–29,* 69, *69*
Hammock, Lazy-Afternoon, 136–39, *137–39*
Handle of hook, 10, *10*
Hat, Mohair Flapper, 100–103, *101–3*
Head of hook, 10, *10*
Hippie Chic Skirt, 114–17, *115–17*
Holding hook and yarn, 20–21, *20–21*
Hook, *10,* 10–11, **11,** 20, *20*

Increase (inc), 69, *69*

Jacket, Designer, 110–13, *111–13*
Jeweled, 118–21, *119–21*
Joining yarn, 32, *32,* 52, *52*

Knots, avoiding, 32

Label on yarn, 41, *41*
Lacy Sleeveless Shell, 74–77, *75–77*

Lamb's wool, 14, *15*
Lampshade Antique Fringe, 132–35, *133–35*
Language of crochet, *18*, 18–19, **19,** 29
Lazy-Afternoon Hammock, 136–39, *137–39*
Left-handers, 140–41, *140–41*
Left-hand side, 18, *18*
Linen yarn, 13
Little Black Wrap, 70–73, *71–73*

Macramé Fringe, 57, *57*
Mercerized cotton yarn, 12
Metric hook sizes, 11, **11**
Microfiber, 17
Mohair Flapper Hat, 100–103, *101–3*
Mohair yarn, 14, *15*
"Motifs" (granny squares), 88–89, *88–89*

Necklaces, 118–21, *119–21*
Novelty yarns, *16*, 17
Nylon yarn, *16*, 17

Parentheses, 19
Pattern, anatomy of, 34–35, *34–35*
Pattern stitches, 52–53, *53*
Pillows
    Diamond Square Pillow, 128–31, *129–31*
    Striped Throw Pillow, 62–65, *63–65*
Pima cotton yarn, 12
Pin, Flower, 91, *91*
Plant fibers, 12–13, *12–13*
Ply and weight of yarn, 17, *17*
Posh Frock, 106–9, *107–9*
Posies for Tanks, 92–95, *93–95*
Post, 18, *18*
Purses (bags)
    Bamboo Handle Purse, 54–57, *55–57*
    Swinging Ribbon Bag, 46–49, *47–49*

Raw silk, 13
Red-Hot Granny Scarf, 96–99, *97–98,* **99**
Ribbon Bag, Swinging, 46–49, *47–49*
Right-hand side, 18, *18*
Right side, 18, *18*

Scarfs
    Basic Scarfs, 42–45, *43–45*
    Red-Hot Granny Scarf, 96–99, *97–98,* **99**
    Striped Skinny Scarf, 58–61, *59–61*
Sea Island cotton yarn, 12
Sewing pieces together, 33, *33*
Shank of hook, 10, *10*
Shaping/fitting, 68–69, *68–69*
Shawl, Little Black Wrap, 70–73, *71–73*
Shell, Lacy Sleeveless, 74–77, *75–77*
Shetland wool, 14, *15*
Silk yarn, 13
Single crochet (sc), 24–25, *24–25,* 68, *68,* 140–41, *140–41*
Sizing, 34
Skirt, Chic Hippie, 114–17, *115–17*
Sleeveless Lacy Shell, 74–77, *75–77*
Slip, Tube, 109, *109*
Slip knot, 21, *21*
Slip stitch (sl st), 69, *69*
Sport weight yarn, 17, *17*
Star symbols, 18–19
Stitches, 24–31
    chain (ch), 22, *22,* 140, *140*
    double crochet (dc), 26–27, *26–27,* 68, *68*
    half double crochet (hdc), 28–29, *28–29,* 69, *69*
    left-handers, 140–41, *140–41*
    pattern, anatomy of, 34
    pattern stitches, 52–53, *53*
    shaping/fitting, 68–69, *68–69*
    single crochet (sc), 24–25, *24–25,* 68, *68,* 140–41, *140–41*

slip stitch (sl st), 69, *69*
triple crochet (tr), 30–31, *30–31*
U. K. (English) terms, 29
Stranding, 52
Stripe (Candy) Baby Sweater, 78–81, *79–81*
Striped Skinny Scarf, 58–61, *59–61*
Striped Throw Pillow, 62–65, *63–65*
Swatches. *See* Gauge
Sweater, Baby Candy Stripe, 78–81, *79–81*
Swimsuit Issue Bikini, 82–85, *83–85*
Swinging Ribbon Bag, 46–49, *47–49*
Symbols, 18–19
Synthetic yarn, *16*, 16–17

Tanks, Posies for, 92–95, *93–95*
Throat of hook, 10, *10*
Triple crochet (tr), 30–31, *30–31*
Tube Slip, 109, *109*
Turning chain, 25, *25*

U. K. hook sizes/terms, 11, **11,** 29
U. S. hook sizes, 11, **11**

Vintage Embellishments, 124–27, *125–27*

Washing instructions, 41, *41*
Weaving in ends, 32, 113, *113*
Weight and ply of yarn, 17, *17*
Wool yarn, 14, *15*
Work even, 18, *18*
Wrap, Little Black, 70–73, *71–73*
Wrong side, 18, *18*

Yarn, 12–17
    animal fibers, 14–15, *14–15*
    holding the yarn, 21, *21*
    hook and, 20
    label, 41, *41*
    plant fibers, 12–13, *12–13*
    synthetics, *16*, 16–17
    weight and ply of yarn, 17, *17*
Yarn over, 18, *18*